# Polikarpov's I-16 Fighter

## Its Forerunners and Progeny

**Yefim Gordon and Keith Dexter**

**Midland Publishing**

**Polikarpov's I-16 Fighter:**
**Its Forerunners and Progeny**
© 2001 Yefim Gordon and Arthur Keith Dexter
ISBN 1 85780 131 8

Published by Midland Publishing
4 Watling Drive, Hinckley, LE10 3EY, England
Tel: 01455 254 490   Fax: 01455 254 495
E-mail: midlandbooks@compuserve.com

Midland Publishing is an imprint of
Ian Allan Publishing Ltd

*Worldwide distribution (except North America):*
Midland Counties Publications
4 Watling Drive, Hinckley, LE10 3EY, England
Telephone: 01455 254 450   Fax: 01455 233 737
E-mail: midlandbooks@compuserve.com
www.midlandcountiessuperstore.com

*North American trade distribution:*
Specialty Press Publishers & Wholesalers Inc.
11605 Kost Dam Road, North Branch, MN 55056
Tel: 651 583 3239   Fax: 651 583 2023
Toll free telephone: 800 895 4585

© 2001 Midland Publishing
Design concept and layout
by Polygon Press Ltd. (Moscow, Russia)
Colour artwork © Sergey Yershov

This book is illustrated with photos from the
archives of Yefim Gordon, Mikhail Maslov and
the Russian Aviation Research Trust

Printed in England by
Ian Allan Printing Ltd
Riverdene Business Park, Molesey Road,
Hersham, Surrey, KT12 4RG

All rights reserved. No part of this
publication may be reproduced,
stored in a retrieval system, transmitted
in any form or by any means, electronic,
mechanical or photo-copied, recorded
or otherwise, without the written
permission of the publishers.

# Contents

| | |
|---|---|
| Introduction | 3 |
| 1. The Ancestors | 5 |
| 2. Enter The I-16 | 13 |
| 3. Version Briefing | 21 |
| 4. Prototypes & Projects – The I-16 in Mass Production | 45 |
| 5. *Ishachok* Anatomy | 57 |
| 6. The I-16 in Action | 61 |
| 7. The 'Super-*Ishachok*' – And Other Successors | 85 |
| Line drawings | 104 |
| Colour drawings | 110 |

Title page: Slogans like this one, *Za SSSR!* (For the USSR!), were common on Soviet fighters during the Great Patriotic War.
Below: Red Banner Baltic Fleet Air Arm pilots and technicians stand in front of their I-16 *tip* 5s. The aircraft were all built at Plant No.39, as evidenced by their black-painted engine cowlings.

# Introduction

Before the Second World War Nikolai Nikolayevich Polikarpov was considered not only to be the principal designer of fighter aircraft in the Soviet Union but was also known as 'the King of Fighters'. However, he had proved to be very versatile and up to 1940 his designs of aircraft of all types and functions were built in greater numbers than those of all other Soviet designers put together. Interestingly, this feat was actually achieved because he was responsible for the development of the U-2, later renamed Polikarpov Po-2, a trainer and general-purpose biplane, prolifically produced over a long period of time; ultimately about 33,000 were built in the Soviet Union, Yugoslavia and Poland during 1928-1955.

Polikarpov was born on the 10th June 1892 in the small village of Georgiyevskoe in the Oryol province and educated at the St. Petersburg Polytechnic Institute. Whilst there he worked in the local office of the Moscow based 'Duks' aircraft manufacturing company. (The name comes from the Latin word *dux*, chief.) On graduating in January 1916 he joined the 'Russo-Baltic Carriage Works' (RBVZ – **Roos**sko-Bal**ti**yskiy Va**gon**nyy Za**vod**) to work under Igor' I. Sikorsky. Five months after the 1917 October Revolution Polikarpov joined the 'Military Air Fleet Board' and by September 1918 was head of the technical department (Tekh**nich**eskiy ot**del**) of 'Duks', a factory located at an airfield in the north-western suburbs of Moscow (now called Khodynka and located right in the heart of the city). Shortly afterwards, in this capacity, he organised production of the British-designed de Havilland D.H.4 and developed it into the R-1 reconnaissance aircraft (R = [samo**lyot**-] raz**ved**chik) of which about 2,800 were ultimately built for the Soviet Air Force. This was not simply a copy of the D.H.4 but a complete redesign incorporating locally available materials, a different engine and also equipment permitting a greater diversity of missions.

The recovery of the Soviet aircraft industry from the ravages of the civil war was slow and painful but in January 1923 an aircraft designer's office (Kon**strook**torskiy ot**del**, KO) was created at the former 'Duks' Moscow factory, now renamed GAZ-1 (Gosoo**dar**stvennyy avi**ats**i**onn**yy za**vod**, state-owned aircraft factory) and Polikarpov was appointed as its chief. His most important task was to design a fighter powered by a 400 hp (298 kW) 'Liberty' engine. This arrangement at GAZ-1 was curtailed by his transfer on the 6th February 1923 to the design office (KO) of Glavkoavia (acronym for the 'Main Management of the Amalgamated Aircraft Factories') and his place in GAZ-1 was taken by Dmitriy P. Grigorovich. However, although the design of the fighter was transferred with Polikarpov it was never built because of a lack of enthusiasm on the part of the management at GAZ-1; a classic case of the 'not invented here' syndrome.

**Acknowledgements**
The authors wish to thank Nigel Eastaway (Russian Aviation Research Trust), Ivan Rodionov, Alexander Boyd, Mikhail Maslov and Dmitriy Komissarov who assisted in making this book.

Nikolai Nikolayevich Polikarpov, the King of Fighters who created the I-16

Above: A cannon-armed I-16 warms up its engine prior to a sortie near Odessa in 1942. The wheel well doors were often missing on operational aircraft.
Below: Thousands of Soviet fighter pilots began their combat careers on the I-16 – an aircraft which participated in four wars (the Spanish Civil War, the Khalkhin-Gol conflict, the Winter War with Finland and the Great Patriotic War).

Chapter 1

# The Ancestors

Polikarpov's first fighter design to be actually built was a monoplane, called the IL-400 (*istrebitel*' [*s **dvig**atelem*] Liberty [***moschn**ost'yu*] 400 [*losha**dinykh** sil*], fighter with a 400-hp Liberty engine) which was completed by August 1923. His decision to use the monoplane layout was, by his own admission, influenced by his examination of a Junkers all-metal monoplane that had been captured during the recently ended Civil War. Although the basic ideas for this project were formulated by the end of 1922 it was not until after he was transferred to the design office of Glavkoavia in February 1923 that Polikarpov had the opportunity to further develop this design. A formal request had been issued by Glavkoavia for a monoplane single seat fighter powered by a 300 hp (224 kW) Hispano-Suiza, a 420 hp (314 kW) Napier or a 400 hp (298kW) Liberty engine. As the aircraft was to be built at GAZ-1, Polikarpov, having learnt from bitter experience that less criticism arose when the management of the factory was directly involved in the project, invited I. M. Kostkin, the production manager, to be joint leader of the project team.

**IL-400** was the designation assigned to this aircraft (also referred to as the IL-400a or IL-1 in later documents); 'I' represented *istrebitel*' (fighter), and L-400 the Liberty 400 hp engine. 'Liberty' was the name given to an engine that, between the years of 1917 and 1919, was mass-produced by six different companies in the USA, with over 20,000 being manufactured, and the engine had a good reputation for reliability. The relationship between the USA and the USSR was strained at this time and there was little or no chance of negotiating an agreement to build the engine under licence. Undeterred, the Soviets went ahead anyway and produced an almost exact copy which they named the M-5 (M for *motor*) but they cleverly side-stepped the licensing regulations by using metric rather than US measurements. Production was in two factories; the first, the Ikar (Icarus) plant in Moscow, known since 1921 as GAZ-2, which merged with GAZ-4 on 2nd March 1927 to become *zavod 24 imeni M. V. Frunze* (named in honour of Mikhail V. Frunze) and the second, the Bol'- shevik plant in what was then Petrograd. This plant was not controlled by Glavkoavia and therefore not numbered in the GAZ list.

The aircraft was constructed of wood and fabric and it had a cantilever wing, the tips of which sloped down at an angle of 3°. Both propeller and radiator were identical to those

**The original IL-400 prototype with GAZ No. 1 engineers posing beside it.**

The wrecked IL-400 after Konstantin K. Artseulov's crash on 16th August 1923.

on the R-1 (Russian-built version of the de Havilland D.H.9a) and the fixed undercarriage had two wire-braced struts per wheel and a joining axle. A fixed tail skid and a tube under each wing-tip afforded protection against damage on landing.

Formal design work on the prototype had started in April 1923 a little in advance of the official go-ahead which was not given until 23rd May. It was built mostly at night to avoid interfering with other work and was completed on 2nd August 1923 thanks to the backing of I. M. Nemtsov, the factory director, and the determined enthusiasm and commitment of Kostkin and Polikarpov. The prototype was not a success; its tail refused to lift, thus rendering the craft incapable of leaving the ground. Moving the undercarriage units back a little and putting 1° anhedral on the horizontal tail enabled the first flight to take place on 16th August 1923. Unfortunately, at a height of 20 m (66 ft) the nose suddenly reared up and after stalling, the aircraft pancaked to the ground, injuring the pilot. At the time it was generally accepted that the cause of the crash was the centre of gravity which was much too far aft, but in his biography of Polikarpov (*Aviakonstrooktor N. N. Polikarpov*), V. P. Ivanov, forwarded the theory that the real villain of the piece was the anhedral applied to the tailplane. This, he suggested, had upset the fighter's stability. A committee of scientists and engineers from the RKKVF (*Raboche-krest'yahnskiy krahsnyy voyenno-vozdooshnyy flot*, Workers' and Peasants' Red Air Fleet) investigated the problem and on 4th October 1923 decided that it would be worthwhile persevering with this design. At Polikarpov's insistence a model was tested in TsAGI (*Tsentrahl'nyy aero-ghidrodinamicheskiy in-stitoot*, Central Aero- and Hydrodynamics Institute) wind tunnel and it was confirmed that the stability would be improved by moving the centre of gravity forward from its original position at 52% to a new one at 30% of the wing chord. These tests overcame the ban on Polikarpov's use of TsAGI facilities occasioned by the rivalry between the managements of GAZ-1 and TsAGI and the animosity between Polikarpov and the deputy Director of TsAGI, Andrey N. Tupolev.

A second prototype known as the **Il-400b** (an abbreviation of *bis*, second or 'Mk 2'), and sometimes referred to as the IL-2, with the centre of gravity moved forward plus a new thinner wing and other refinements, took to the air for the first time on 18th July 1924 and after 25 test flights an order for a pre-production batch of eight was placed with GAZ-1. On the fuselage of the Il-400b was painted the slogan **Kryl'ya mirovoy kommoony GAZ No.1 imeni ODVF** (Wings of the World Commune, State Aviation Factory No.1 named after the ODVF); the ODVF (*Obshchestvo droozey vozdooshnovo flota*) was a paramilitary civilian support group for the Soviet Air Force.

A top speed of 263 km/h (164 mph) had been achieved and the IL-400b was said to handle neatly and respond quickly, but it was criticised for the heaviness of its flight controls.

Polikarpov returned to GAZ-1 in August 1924 as head of its KB (*Konstrooktorskoye byuro*, design bureau) and State Acceptance Tests of the IL-400b started on 17th October 1924. In early February 1925, after the engine had been replaced, the prototype was demonstrated to P. I. Baranov, recently appointed Commander in Chief of the Soviet Air Force. He authorised the necessary expenditure to allow GAZ-1 to build a pre-production batch of eight aeroplanes. It is worth noting that from 1st January 1925 the Soviet Air Force had been renamed *Voyenno-Vozdooshnyye Seely Raboche-Krest'yahnskoy Krahsnoy Armii*, the Military Air Force of the Workers' and Peasants' Red Army.

**I-1** (I for *Istrebitel'*, fighter) was the VVS designation of the production version of IL-400b, for which an order of 25 had been placed, and was known to the factory as the IL-3. Aviatrest, which had replaced Glavkoavia on 28th January 1925, insisted in a letter to GAZ-1 that from 18th June 1926 this aircraft should be referred to only as the I-1. By this measure it was intended to put an end to the confusion that had arisen from the plethora of designations attached to this type.

Although trials went reasonably well other unfortunate events, were to influence the fate

**Data for the IL-400b***

| Span | 10.8 m (35.4 ft) |
|---|---|
| Length | 8.2 m (26.9 ft) |
| Wing area | 20.0 m² (215 ft²) |
| Weight empty | 1,112 kg (2,451 lb) |
| Gross weight | 1,510 kg (3,329 lb) |
| Maximum speed at sea level | 274 km/h (170 mph) |
| Maximum speed at height | 280 km/h (174 mph) |
| Climb to 1,000 m | 1.9 min |
| Climb to 5,000 m | 15 min |
| Ceiling | 7,400 m (24,280 ft) |
| Endurance | 2.5 hrs |
| Time to turn 360 | 19 sec |
| Landing speed | 100 km/h (62 mph) |
| Landing run time | 15 sec |
| Take-off run time | 8 sec |

* Only one prototype of which was built and that at GAZ-1 imeni ODVF.

The sole IL-400b. The inscription on the fuselage reads *Kryl'ya mirovoy kommoony – GAZ No.1 imeni ODVF* (The wings of the World Commune – GAZ No. 1 named after the Air Fleet Friends' Society).

of the I-1. On 31st March 1926 during the testing of the Polikarpov 2I-N1 biplane escort fighter, test pilot Filippov and his observer V. V. Mikhailov were both killed. The skin covering of the upper starboard wing had torn away, causing the collapse of both wings at a height of 100 m (328 ft). The principal reason for the crash was defective bonding of the wing skin and structure. Although this was shown to be purely a result of manufacturing deficiencies, the Aviatrest technical section also expressed doubts about the rigidity of the wing structure. Not only were their observations aimed at the 2I-N1 but also at the I-1 whose wings were of a similar design. There was some ground for their concern because the new standards introduced in 1925 covering these features had not yet been met.

Evaluation tests of the I-1 were halted and production stopped. Wingless fuselages stood forlornly on the production lines of GAZ-1 while experts argued over what was to be done. Although only thirty-three I-1s had been ordered, it had originally been intended to extend the number to eighty. That figure was then reduced to twelve and a decision taken not to continue further development of the I-1 or of its derivatives. A production I-1 (construction number 2891) was found to have a top speed of 295 km/h (183 mph) at height and took 17 minutes to climb to 5000 m (about 16,700 ft). The aircraft was designated to be flown only by skilled pilots and an I-1 was specially modified to allow safe adjustment of ballast to reproduce and assess the efficiency and safety of a range of centre of gravity positions. It was found that instability occurred when the centre of gravity was positioned at anything greater than 35.0% of wing chord and that 32.5% gave the best handling characteristics.

**Data for the I-1***

| Span | 10.8 m (35.4 ft) |
|---|---|
| Length | 7.7 m (25.3 ft) |
| Height with the taller rudder | 3.1 m (10.2 ft) |
| Wing area | 20 m² (215 ft²) |
| Take-off weight | 1,500 kg (3,308 lb) |
| Maximum speed at sea level | 273 km/h (170 mph) |
| Maximum speed at height | 295 km/h (183 mph) |
| Climb to 1,000m | 2.5 min |
| Climb to 2,000 m | 4.75 min |
| Climb to 5,000 m | 17 min |
| Time to turn 360 | 20 sec |
| Landing speed | 75 km/h (47 mph) |
| Landing run time | 7 sec |
| Take-off run time | 6 sec |

* As measured on the aircraft with construction number 2891.

The 1920s was a decade of great transition in the aircraft industry as attempts were made to find the most effective blend of capable staff and appropriate organisation structures and it was during this period, in August 1924, that Polikarpov had been transferred from Glavkoavia back to GAZ-1 in the Khodynka area of Moscow. His new role encompassed the jobs of production manager and head of the factory design office (***Op**ytnyy ot**del*** GAZ-1, Experimental Department of the State Aircraft Factory Number 1) where he replaced Grigorovich. To improve the efficiency of the design office he split it into several sections each being given a clear task for which the section chief was accountable. A new law had been enacted from 11th September 1924 specifying the rights of originators of industrial inventions. As the team jointly lead by Polikarpov and Kostkin had seven other members who could also claim part ownership of this 'invention', it was unanimously decided to attribute ownership to GAZ-1, thus allowing the factory free rights over the series-produced aircraft. Any other decision would have involved lengthy and no doubt acrimonious legal proceedings. However, Polikarpov was recognised by the powers-that-be as the instigator of, and driving force behind, this project.

The projected **IL-4**, also referred to as **I-6** and **IL-400v**, was intended to replace the I-1 on the production lines of GAZ-1. Work on this model commenced in the autumn of 1925 and it was formally accepted by the factory on 30th November 1925. It was an improved version of the I-1 with a longer wingspan and greater wing area to improve manoeuvrability and climb rate at the expense of a slight reduction in top speed. The cockpit was to be moved forward by 50 cm (19.7 in.) to improve the pilot's view and four spars in the wing construction increased the strength. All fuel was to be carried in the wings. However, the most remarkable feature of this design was its versatility. There were to be three variants: single and two seat fighters both called IL-400v and a reconnaissance aircraft, the RL-400v (*raz**v**ed*chik [s ***dvig**atelem*] Liberty [***mosch**nost'yu*] 400 [*loshadinykh sil*]). The letter 'v' is not an abbreviation but, as it is, the third letter of the Cyrillic alphabet; it denotes the third variant of the IL-400 design. All versions were to be interchangeable in the field. However, this versatility was not considered realistic; only the single-seater was accepted by the Aviatrest and work began on the prototype. Second

Above: The IL-400b after coming to grief on landing.

Left: Close-up of the overturned IL-400b; the propeller appears to have suffered no damage. Note the torn wing skin.

Below: Three-quarters rear view of the IL-400b following repairs, showing to advantage the corrugated skin. Note that the fuselage slogan has been restyled.

thoughts in February 1926 resulted in further work being halted until the IL-3 (I-1) had been built. The programme was finally abandoned on 26th April.

**Projected data for the IL-400v**

| | |
|---|---|
| Span (single-seater) | 11.7 m (38.4 ft) |
| Span (two-seat fighter) | 14.0 m (46.0 ft) |
| Span (RL-400v) | 16.2 m (53.1 ft) |
| Length (single-seat fighter) | 7.8 m (25.6 ft) |
| Length (two-seat fighter) | 9.0 m (29.5 ft) |
| Length (RL-400v) | 9.0 m (29.5 ft) |
| Take-off weight (single-seater) | 1,650 kg (3,638 lb) |
| Max speed (single-seater) at sea level) | 260 km/h (162 mph) |
| Service ceiling (single-seater) | 7,400 m (24,280 ft) |
| Climb to 2,000 m (single-seater) | 4 min |
| Endurance | 2.5 hrs |

Reorganisations were also taking place at national level (trusts had become the favoured organisation for control of industries) and led to the replacement of Glavkoavia by Aviatrest on the 7th January 1925. This was accompanied shortly after by the creation of a combined design office and experimental department headed by Polikarpov. It was known as the OSS (*Otdel sookhoputnykh samolyotov*, landplane department) of the Central Design Bureau (TsKB, *Tsentrahl'noye konstrooktorskoye byuro*). Some sources suggest the name was OO (*Opytnyy otdel*, experimental department) and was still based at GAZ-1. Whichever was the case, by October 1926 this had become OPO-1 (a different acronym for the same meaning as OO) of TsKB, Aviatrest.

In the many design departments of which Polikarpov was head about 40 aircraft projects were completed between 1924 and the end of 1928, and even though few were built his prestige was greatly enhanced by this fecundity. He had even been permitted to visit Britain, France, Germany and Holland to study the methodology of their aircraft industries.

To accelerate the speed of new developments *zavod* 25, also at Khodynka, was set up to accommodate OPO-1 and to provide it with dedicated production facilities. Polikarpov brought in his team on 24th February 1928 and was additionally appointed Deputy Director of the factory. Note that the aircraft plants were no longer called GAZ but had been renumbered in 1927 into a list of defence plants and each was now referred to as a '*Gosoodarstvennyy soyooznyy zavod*' (State union factory) or zavod for short. (The 'union' part meant that it had national importance.) Confusingly, a GAZ number from then onwards referred to automobile plants or their production models!

In September 1929 Polikarpov was arrested, falsely accused of being an industrial saboteur and condemned to death as an *enemy of the people* but the sentence was commuted to 10 years imprisonment in a labour camp. Many other aircraft designers, including Grigorovich, suffered a similar fate. In December 1929 a group of them, including Polikarpov, was brought together in Butyrka prison, Moscow, and under the supervision of Goriyanov of the OGPU, was set to work to design aircraft with Grigorovich as chief designer. It later transpired that this was a

One of the I-1 fighters. This example appears to be painted olive drab overall, except for the cowling.

Above and below: A production I-1. These views illustrate well the smooth skin, ventral radiator, longer nose and recontoured vertical tail of the production version (compare this aircraft with the example on the previous page).

blatant attempt by the OGPU to demonstrate that repression was the best motivation and the most effective way to maintain control of the industry. 'KB **Vnoot**rennyaya tyur'**ma**' (VT), Internal Prison Design Bureau, was the name given to this team and in January 1930, they were moved to hangar number 7 in the grounds of za**vod** 39 i**men**i V. P. Menzhinsko-vo (named after V. P. Menzhinskiy). This factory was also located in the Khodynka area. At first the team was led by D. P. Grigorovich but it was not long before he gave way to Polikarpov whose fighter design, the future I-5, had been preferred over a design suggestion of Grigorovich.

Further wholesale reorganisation took place on 3rd March 1930 when Aviatrest and the other defence trusts were abolished and replaced on 16th April 1930 by 'All-Union Associations or Ob"yedi**neni**ya of which one, the VAO (Vseso**yoo**znoye aviatsi**on**noye ob"yedi**nen**iye, All-union Aviation Association), was devoted to aviation and controlled by the Ministry of War. The next change was the absorption of zavod 25 by zavod 39 in August 1930 and the merging of the design teams from zavody 22 and 28 into TsKB,VAO. At the same time the Polikarpov and the other designers of the KB VT became part of the TsKB, VAO but remained under OGPU control.

Polikarpov's luck changed for the better in June 1931 when Stalin was favourably impressed by the performance of the I-5 and observations which Polikarpov made at the Aviation Review which took place at the Central Airfield at Khodynka. Subsequently, on 7th July 1931 Polikarpov and some of his colleagues were granted an amnesty which gave them their freedom but the 'guilty' verdicts were not quashed until 1st September 1956 by which time it was too late to benefit Polikarpov who had died on 30th July 1944.

The **I-11** monoplane single-seat fighter project was conceived by Polikarpov after he had been released from the KB VT, of the OGPU in July 1931

It was was developed in response to a VVS request in 1932 for a single seat fighter with a metal airframe and a high top speed. The recently developed policy was to field a mixed force of agile biplanes and very fast monoplane fighters.

The only other fact known about this project was that the power was to be from a Mikulin M-34F. Even this snippet seems implausible because that particular in-line engine was unavailable until 1935, by which time Polikarpov was heavily involved with the I-16.

The number of experimental departments (OPOs) each of which had a design team had constantly been increased at TsKB, VAO. There were 10 OPOs by September 1931 when TsAGI took control of TsKB VAO and merged it with its own experimental team, AGOS (avi**ah**tsiya, **ghid**roavi**ah**tsiya i **op**yt-noye stroi**tel**'stvo – Aviation, hydro-aviation and experimental [aircraft] construction).

A design team within TsKB, TsAGI was known as a 'bri**gah**da' (brigade) and Polikarpov was given charge of Brigade No.3, a post which he lost when he refused A. N. Tupolev's request to design all-metal aircraft. It is likely that this reluctance on Polikarpov's part to become involved in this project originated from his conviction that Soviet aircraft should be built as far as possible from locally sourced material in plentiful supply, ie, wood. For a time Polikarpov worked as Pavel O. Sukhoi's deputy but in order to achieve the directive of producing two fighters, a monoplane and a biplane. By mid-1933 two fighter design brigades were formed; Polikarpov was appointed head of brigade No.5 which was tasked with developing the biplane fighter.

Ob"yedineniya soon fell out of favour and on 5th January 1932 VAO was replaced by GUAP (**Glav**noye oo**prav**l**en**iye aviatsi**on**noy pro**mysh**lennosti, Main Directorate of the Aviation Industry). As a result a reorganisation further down the line took place in January 1933 when the TsKB, although remaining at zavod 39, was separated from TsAGI. For this reason it was frequently referred to as TsKB-39 as well as its official title TsKB, GUAP. Sergey V. Il'yushin was appointed both Chief Designer and Deputy Factory Director and oversaw five airframe and two aircraft equipment brigades. Polikarpov was in charge of Brigade No.2 which was to specialise in the design and manufacture of fighter prototypes.

At a conference of the aviation industry and its customers in August 1935 Polikarpov was congratulated on his fighter designs and he took advantage of the occasion to express concern over the physical separation of design offices from the series production plants and also of the lamentable lack of modern experimental facilities. His comments were well received and it was decided to base as many design teams as possible in series production plants and to give each team its own experimental facilities. The result was the decentralisation of aircraft designing and the formation in 1936 of a number of **Opytno-kon-strook**torskoye by**uro** (OKBs), Experimental Design Bureaux based at aircraft factories. It was intended that the OKBs should compete with one another to develop an aircraft prototype with the view that the favoured one would then be mass-produced at their base factory. In this way the factory would have a strong incentive to co-operate with the OKB. Such was the prestige of Polikarpov, by now called 'the king of fighters', that on 5th June 1936 he was appointed Chief Designer of two OKBs, at zavody 21 in Gor'kiy (now Nizhniy Novgorod) and 84 in Khimki near Moscow.

In 1937 Polikarpov and his OKB were transferred to the TsAGI plant for experimental designs known as ZOK (Za**vod** **op**ytnykh kon**strook**tsiy). This was located at zavod 156 in Moscow where, after reviewing a range of projects with optimistic performance estimates, he settled down to build the I-180 fighter, a development of the I-16. KB-2 zavoda 156 was specially formed to expedite progress of this design. Unfortunately the first prototype crashed but, when it was established that it was not a design fault, plans went ahead to build a second prototype. In February 1939 the OKB was transferred to zavod 1 and it was there that the second prototype was built but this, too, crashed due to a failure of the engine oil cooler. By this time Polikarpov's star was on the wane and a new generation of fighter designers headed by Aleksandr S. Yakovlev was exciting attention. After a visit to Germany, Polikarpov returned to find that a second design group, then an OKO, with Artyom I. Mikoyan in charge had been formed in zavod 1. Furthermore it had taken over the development of the I-400 (the future MiG-1), a design initiated by Polikarpov as Samolyot Kh (aircraft Kh; 'kh', the 22nd letter of the Russian alphabet, was an in-house product code). Unable to reclaim his progeny and having lost eighty of his design staff to the new team, Polikarpov moved in July 1940 a short distance to zavod 51 as Director and Chief Designer.

Zavod 51 was not the large plant it is today but a hangar which once housed the production workshops of TsAGI's 8th Department. It was located in a fenced-off region within the site of zavod 1 at Khodynka. The OKB was intensively engaged in drawing up more fighter designs there when the German invasion necessitated evacuation to Novosibirsk in October 1941. As zavod 153 was already full the OKB used the Oblavtotrans car repair base at nearby Tolmachovo airfield. Work continued at this site on the I-185 fighter, as well as gliders and other types, and carried on after the return to zavod 51 in July 1943. Regrettably this fighter was rejected and, although terminally ill with cancer, Nikolai Polikarpov, with unflagging enthusiasm, worked on many new designs including one for a projected rocket fighter the Mal**yut**ka (Baby) until his death on 30th July 1944.

Above and below: The I-14, seen here with a ski undercarriage, was the chief competitor of the future I-16. The aircraft, which was designed by Pavel O. Sukhoi when he was still chief of a design team at Andrey N. Tupolev's OKB, did enter production but on a much smaller scale.

Chapter 2

# Enter The I-16

The I-16 was the *pièce de resistance* of Nikolai Polikarpov and was the first monoplane fighter in the world to enter service with a retractable undercarriage and enclosed cockpit. It was only for a short time that the Soviet Air Force could claim a world beater because in 1935 the Hawker Hurricane and Messerschmitt Bf 109 took to the air. In one respect it was unfortunate that the I-16 was kept in production as a fighter until 1941. By this time it had become obsolescent and many lives had been sacrificed in battle by its inadequacy against the more advanced enemy machines.

One of the most difficult decisions that wartime leaders had to take was when to replace an existing model by a more modern design. The trade-off between loss of production during the changeover and the advantages of the new product was difficult to assess and depended on the state of the war at that time; therefore, it is easy to be critical with the benefit of hindsight.

During the time that Polikarpov was working as deputy to Pavel O. Sukhoi, leader of Brigade No.3 in 1932, he sketched out the first details of the future I-16. In 1933 as head of Brigade No.2 in the TsKB, now independent of TsAGI, he began work in earnest on the new monoplane fighter. He tackled his first problem of obtaining official backing by forging a good relationship with the head of the VVS Yakov I. Alksnis and persuading him that the new fighter was his idea. Polikarpov's prestige was at an all-time high since he had designed the I-3 and I-5 fighters, the latter being a particular favourite of the Commander-in-Chief. Not officially listed in the official budget, the monoplane was nonetheless introduced in the approved design schedule

**Front and rear views of the M-22-powered first prototype I-16 (TsKB-12) on skis in the TsKB yard. The aircraft was bright red overall.**

13

The TsKB-12 on wheels, with the cockpit canopy fully open. This view shows to advantage the characteristic cowling design of the M-22 powered versions.

as the **TsKB-12**, the digits indicating it was the twelfth design to emanate from the Central Design Bureau.

With its stocky barrel-shaped fuselage, low cantilever wing and large tail it was intended to have the smallest dimensions and lightest weight that could meet the requirements of the VVS. Its centre of gravity was at just over 30% of wing chord in order to improve manoeuvrability. On the other hand, this made it somewhat unstable, ie twitchy, in flight and thus difficult to fly; however, this was considered a reasonable trade-off. Polikarpov favoured a radial engine because it was lighter than the liquid-cooled in-line type and was less susceptible to battle damage. He considered this more than adequate compensation for the extra drag from its greater frontal area. The first choice of engine was the 700 hp (523 kW) Wright R-1820 Cyclone for which negotiations to license its building in the USSR were underway. As this engine was unlikely to be available in time, Alksnis persuaded Polikarpov that the 480 hp (358 kW) M-22, a Soviet-built version of the Bristol Jupiter VI, would suffice as an interim measure and give the desired top speed of over

The first prototype at the airfield of the Kacha Flying School near Sevastopol' in the spring of 1934.

Above: The TsKB-12 trestled for landing gear retraction tests.

Another view of the TsKB-12 on skis, with Valeriy P. Chkalov in the cockpit. Note the new three-bladed Hamilton Standard propeller.

*The first prototype TsKB-12 following a crash-landing. Despite the fact that relatively little damage is visible, the aircraft was declared a write-off.*

300 km/h (186 mph) at 5,000 m. It was proposed to fit a NACA cowling after tests indicated that it was aerodynamically more efficient than a Townend ring.

Polikarpov pursued his ambition of obtaining the more powerful Wright Cyclone as he wanted his new fighter to achieve at least 400 km/h (250 mph). When he succeeded in purchasing the low-altitude rated 600 hp (447 kW) Cyclone R-1820F-2 he was permitted to build two prototypes utilising both it and the M-22. Work had started in earnest at the TsKB from June 1933 and by the end of that year both were ready for their first flight. As this was the depth of winter, fixed ski undercarriages were used to avoid delaying tests until the spring thaw.

When making decisions about the type of materials to be used in the construction of the TsKB-12, Polikarpov sensibly elected to employ materials readily available in a not yet fully industrialised Soviet Union. As suitable metals were in short supply the all-metal stressed skin fuselage favoured by Western designers was not an option and wood, which was in plentiful supply, became the dominant material. A forward-sliding cockpit canopy was installed, with a downward-hinged door on the port side. Unfortunately, with time, the canopy was likely to become opaque and consequently was usually left open. The pilot's seat was made of duralumin and had a recess for the parachute.

All the tail surfaces were of duralumin structure covered with fabric and the vertical tail off-set 2° to balance the propeller's torque. Complications arose from the opposite airscrew rotations of the M-22 and the Wright Cyclone engines. This problem was resolved by the ingenious design of the tailfin which enabled it to be adjusted when the aircraft was on the ground to accommodate either direction of propeller torque. The wing had a centre section and two detachable outer panels. Most of the load bearing was accomplished by two stainless steel spars which, as they were widely separated, were given rigidity by connecting them with duralumin ribs and tubular struts. The outer wing panels had a similar structure and were joined to the centre section by tubular fittings with threaded outer sections. Where the centreplane joined the fuselage the skinning was plywood up to the second rib after which it was duralumin and this alloy was used in 10cm wide bands to cover the gaps between outer wings and centreplane. Strips of duralumin were used to protect the leading edges, but fabric was used to cover the rest of the wings. Although no flaps were installed, both ailerons could be lowered simultaneously as a substitute.

*The third I-16 built by aircraft factory No. 39 in 1934 (c/n 123903) – still powered by an M-22. The aircraft has '3 с' (i.e., '3 s' in Cyrillic characters, meaning tretiy seriynyy [samolyot], third production aircraft) chalked on the rudder. Note the main gear doors fitted to production aircraft*

I-16 c/n 123903 with the engine running.

A unique feature of this fighter was its retractable main undercarriage actuated by a hand crank on the starboard side of the cockpit. This handle so resembled that of a barrel-organ that it was given the Russian name for this instrument, *sharmahnka*. Turning it was extremely hard work and 44 (!) revolutions were needed for the retraction. When retracted, the wheels nestled in wells situated between the centre section spars. A fixed tail skid was used.

Armament was not initially fitted but later two 7.62 mm ShKAS machine guns ([*poole-myot*] *Shpital'novo i Komarnitskovo, aviat-sionnyy, skorostrel'nyy* – Shpital'nyy & Komarnitskiy Fast-Firing Aircraft Gun), each with 900 rounds, were installed in the wings to fire outside of the propeller disc. Sighting was through an 'Aldis' type sight known in the Soviet Union as the OP-1 (*opticheskiy pritsel*); this comprised a tube inside which was a grid.

The first flight of the M-22 version was undertaken by Valeriy P. Chkalov on 30th December 1933 and that of the second prototype with the Cyclone engine followed early in the new year. As expected, the aircraft was proclaimed both complicated and difficult to fly with tricky handling characteristics. Modifications were made during the Factory Test period to improve matters and both aircraft were despatched for State Acceptance Tests at the NII VVS (*Naoochno-issle-dovatel'skiy institoot Voyenno-Vozdoosh-nykh Sil*, Research Institute of the Air Force).

The tests started on 16th February 1934 with Vladimir K. Kokkinaki flying the M-22 variant and V. Stepanchonok the aircraft having the Cyclone engine. Later, pilots Yumashev and Chernavskiy also became involved in the tests. Incidentally, a decision had already been taken on 22nd November 1933 by the STO (*Sovet troodah i oborony*, Soviet Council for Labour and Defence) to put the TsKB-12 into series production at two plants: *zavod* 21 at Gor'kiy, now renamed back to Nizhniy Novgorod, and *zavod 39 imeni V. R. Menzhinsko-vo*, home of the TsKB at Khodynka. This move not only showed faith in the TsKB-12 but put great pressure on all concerned to justify that faith!

The OP-1 optical gunsight and the cockpit canopy in the fully open position.

Preliminary tests were completed by 26th February and the aircraft returned to the TsKB for any faults to be remedied and wheeled undercarriages to be fitted. It was agreed that the new fighter was difficult to fly; in fact, aerobatics were forbidden at this stage. The biggest problem was in landing the aircraft, as it could not be levelled out until very close to the ground but it was reported to have a good level speed, acceptable stability on all three axes and adequate manoeuvrability. A recommendation was made to replace the Cyclone R-1820F-2 with the F-3 model.

Polikarpov was still dogged by the lingering animosity of TsAGI's management whose aerodynamicists A. Zhooravchenko and V. Pyshnov now took to criticising his brainchild, the TsKB-12, predicting that it would fall into a flat spin and fail to recover unless its tail plane was raised. They favoured its competitor, the I-14 designed by P. O. Sukhoi under the patronage of A. N. Tupolev. This rival fighter was equally tricky to fly and it, too, had the weakness of being very difficult to recover from a spin. At two conferences on 17th January and 21st February 1934 arguments raged and it was decided to put the TsKB-12 to a flight test. Chkalov spun the aircraft safely seventy-five times on 1st and 2nd March, easily extricating himself from that manoeuvre by simply centralising the controls and there

The third prototype TsKB-12 at the NII VVS airfield in Schcholkovo (1934) with the canopy closed. This view illustrates well the redesigned cowling of the Wright Cyclone with individual exhaust stubs and the conical propeller spinner. The main gear doors are still missing at this stage.

was no tendency whatever for it to go into a flat spin. While this triumph vindicated Polikarpov and his supporters, it embittered his opponents still further and they continued to snipe at the type on every possible occasion.

Shortly after the spin trials the two prototypes were sent to Kacha, near Sevastopol', where climatic conditions were more suitable and the State Acceptance Tests continued from 22nd March. The physically exhausting manual retraction of the undercarriage caused the biggest problem by distracting the pilot's attention from other important tasks; the undercarriage on the Cyclone-powered prototype was therefore left unretracted. On 14th April failure of the lock on the port leg damaged the aircraft sufficiently for it to be returned to the factory for repairs. Tests on the M-22 powered prototype were completed the following week and it was flown back to Moscow by Chkalov in time to make a triumphant flight over Red Square in formation with the Polikarpov I-15 biplane and the Tupolev I-14 monoplane fighters. Meanwhile tests continued at Kacha with the Cyclone prototype until 25th April.

The trials at Kacha produced some favourable reports. Kokkinaki flew the M-22 engined aircraft when it weighed 1,312 kg (2,894 lb.). At this weight and with wheels

The same aircraft with the canopy fully open.

18

**Production I-16 *tip* 4 fighters during final assembly at aircraft factory No. 39.**

retracted he achieved a maximum speed of 359 km/h (223 mph) at sea level and 325 km/h (201mph) at 5,000 m (16,400 ft). This demonstrated that, despite an engine of elderly design and low power, this aircraft was only slightly inferior to the foreign competition in top speed at 5,000 m (16,400 ft), superior up to 2,000 m (6,500 ft) and as good, if not better, than any for rate of climb and service ceiling. When compared with the Polikarpov I-15 biplane fighter then in service with the VVS it was faster by 80 km/h (49 mph) at 5,000 m (16,400 ft). It was, therefore, no surprise when Alksnis ordered the M-22 version into immediate series production in spite of its shortcomings. He did, however, stipulate that the faults should first be rectified and the head of the NII VVS, V. Konart, was made personally responsible for monitoring progress on their elimination. As a recommendation was made that only average or better-than-average pilots be allowed to fly this type, Alksnis instructed his staff to develop a selection and training scheme guaranteeing that only first-rate pilots flew the TsKB-12, now designated by the VVS as the I-16.

In the course of repairing the Cyclone-powered aircraft damaged on the 14th April, the TsKB not only changed and strengthened the undercarriage retraction gear but also fitted a new 640 hp (477 kW) Wright Cyclone R-1820F-3 with a tunnel cowling having its trailing edge flush with the fuselage and provision for nine exhaust stacks. Its wings were also strengthened. A spinner was added to the two-blade propeller that had replaced the original three-blade Hamilton 'Standard'. As a finishing touch the aeroplane was highly polished. At this time no action was taken to modify the troublesome manual retraction of the undercarriage.

Further tests were carried out on this aircraft at the NII VVS airfield by Kokkinaki and produced the following data:

| | |
|---|---|
| Span | 9.0 m (29.5 ft) |
| Length | 5.9 m (19.2 ft) |
| Height | 3.25 m (10.7 ft) |
| Wing area | 14.54 m$^2$ (1,56.5 ft$^2$) |
| Weight empty | 1,040 kg (2,293 lb) |
| Maximum take-off weight | 1,420 kg (3,131 lb) |
| Maximum speed: | |
|   at sea level | 362 km/h (224 mph) |
|   at 3,000 m | 437 km/h (271 mph) |
|   at 5,000 m | 413 km/h (256 mph) |
| Climb to 5,000 m | 6.8 min |
| Service ceiling | 8,800 m (28,870 ft) |
| Landing speed | 110 km/h (68 mph) |

**The famous Soviet test pilot Valeriy P. Chkalov, Hero of the Soviet Union, tested most of the I-16's variants.**

A curious collection of development aircraft (and competitors, as it were) at NII VVS in Schcholkovo (the airbase which is now called Chkalovskaya), with an I-14 and a Polikarpov I-153 biplane flanked by two I-16s. The far I-16 carries the letters 'IE' on the rudder meaning that the aircraft belongs to the People's Comissariat of Aviation Industry. The machine in the foreground appears to be a captured Nakajima Ki-27.

Chapter 3

# Version Briefing

*Zavod 39 imeni V. R. Menzhinskovo* was the first factory to start series production of the I-16 in 1934 and in that year fifty were built. M-22 engines were installed as supplies of the Soviet built version of the Wright Cyclone R-1820F-3, designated the M-25, were not yet available. It was a tradition that all aircraft manufactured by *zavod* 39 left the factory with their cowlings painted black. Mass-produced aircraft incorporated the modifications of the rebuilt second prototype except for the engine and an 8 mm (0.5 in.) thick armoured seat for the pilot. Construction numbers of these I-16s had six digits: the first two were always 12 to indicate TsKB-12, the twelfth design of the TsKB which was based at this plant; the next two digits were always 39 the *zavod* number and the last two were in sequential order starting at 01 and continuing, in this case, to 50. Thus the first series-produced I-16 had the construction number 123901.

*Zavod* 21 at Gor'kiy, now Nizhniy Novgorod, had received all the blueprints by April 1934 to enable it to start production of the I-16. However, none were produced there that year because it took several months to complete the changes necessary to shift production to the new fighter and it was not until early 1935 that the first I-16 came off the production line. In all, 527 were built in 1935.

**I-16 *tip* 4**, i.e. type 4, indicates that this was the 4th type of aircraft built at *zavod* 21 but this designation was also used for the M-22 engined I-16s series produced at *zavod* 39. Therefore *tip* 4 was the first variant to enter service, the prototypes being known as TsKB-12. Designations I-16 *tip* 1, 2 and 3 were not used.

*Zavod* 21 was seen as the main series production plant for this type; in fact, it went on to build 8,494. Eight more, four in 1935 and a further four in 1936, were assembled by the experimental plant *zavod* 39 but these were special. At some time in 1935 *zavod* 21 changed over to the M-22 engine and records for this do not differentiate between the two variants; consequently it is not known how many of the 527 built were *tip* 4s and how many represented the next model, *tip* 5.

In November 1934, having heard contradictory reports about the I-16, Iosif V. Stalin decided to make up his own mind at first hand and, with a high-powered entourage, descended on Khodynka airfield. Test pilot Chkalov put on a special display and, in trying to lower a reluctant retracted undercarriage, exhibited some very spirited manoeuvres before the mechanism fell into place and he could land. Stalin, not knowing the reason for these pyrotechnics, was so impressed with both pilot and aircraft and also with the lavish praises that the other pilots heaped upon the aircraft, that he ordered the formation of an aerobatic team – Polikarpov now had a very powerful champion.

Five specially lightened I-16s were built at *zavod* 39 with imported Wright Cyclone R-1820F-3 engines and painted red with a black cowling and delivered in March 1935. The pilots were Kokkinaki (the team's leader), Shevchenko, Sooproon, Yevseyev, Preman and occasionally Chkalov. The 'Red Five' performed regularly at flypasts and airshows,

**An I-16 *tip* 4 operated by a flying school, with a Polikarpov R-Z reconnaissance biplane in the background.**

Above and below: The prototype I-16 *tip* 5 (c/n 123954). The 'A 4' tail markings are probably a 'racing number', since the aircraft was one of five I-16s operated by the 'Red Five' display team.

Above: An I-16 *tip* 5 during State acceptance trials at NII VVS, as evidenced by the characteristic hexagonal pavement blocks.

Below: A production I-16 *tip* 5 (c/n 521021); note the hole beneath the star insignia on the fuselage, apparently torn by a bomb fragment.

An I-16 *tip* 5 with bombs on the wing racks during armament trials at NII VVS.

earning for themselves great prestige as well as such mundane rewards as cash and a car each. Their most famous manoeuvre was a slow climbing roll from ground level executed by the whole group. The team were also sent on tour of VVS airfields to put on a display which would demonstrate to service pilots the capabilities of the I-16. This exercise was successful in repudiating its reputation for being almost impossible to fly and built confidence in the type.

The Soviet government was so proud of the I-16 that it was exhibited at the Milan International Air Show in October 1935. Earlier that year in May Stalin had shown off his 'Red Five' display team to the French Minister M. Lavalle who was so impressed with the performance that he organised a similar aerobatic team on his return to France.

The **I-16 *tip* 5 (I-16 M-25A)** was the next version to be mass-produced at *zavod* 21. Advantage was taken of the licence agreement to start building the Wright Cyclone R-1820F-3 in 1934 at the newly constructed plant *zavod* 19 *imeni Stalina* at Perm' in the Urals. This new 730 hp (545 kW) engine was designated M-25A by the Soviets and, using some imported parts, the factory built 660 in 1935. Before series production started at *zavod* 21, acceptance tests for *tip* 5 were carried out using one of the famous 'Red Fives', construction number 123954, which had been built by *zavod* 39. In November 1936, when full-scale production was already under way, an example was tested at the NII VVS; A. Nikashin and Ye. Preman were the test pilots employed. These trials showed that although weight had increased to 1,508 kg (3,325 lb) compared with 1,354 kg (2,986 lb), top speed had risen from 362 km/h (226 mph) to 390 km/h (242 mph) at sea level and from 346 km/h (215 mph) to 445 km/h (276 mph) at

A production I-16 *tip* 5 with the spinner removed.

Above: An I-16 *tip* 5 with an experimental cylindrical centreline drop tank during trials at NII VVS.

Right: An I-16 *tip* 5 on skis with an experimental conformal drop tank.

Below: The same aircraft as it jettisons the drop tank. The skis are apparently non-retractable.

Above and below: I-16 *tip* 5 '7 Red' was used for long-range radio trials by NII VVS. It is seen here prior to installation of the radio.

3,000m (1,900 ft) but the rate of climb and range had deteriorated compared with *tip* 4.

Other changes built into *tip* 5 were: a strengthened structure, the addition of a starter motor, installation of an oxygen system and the fitting of yet another undercarriage retraction system, albeit still hand-cranked. This variant stayed in production until 1939 and several more modifications were introduced piecemeal by the factory. For example, larger 700x150 mm mainwheels and shorter ailerons were phased in and the sliding part of the canopy discarded. Furthermore, it had been reported by service and test pilots that the wing fabric bulged at times of extreme stress, and to counter this fault extra wing ribs were added.

In order to silence once and for all criticism from service pilots of the spin behaviour of the I-16 five NII VVS test pilots executed more than 3,000 successful manoeuvres of this type on series-produced aircraft.

It was this variant that was sent first to help the Republican, i.e. government, side in the Spanish Civil War and it was the Spaniards who christened the I-16 *Mosca* (fly); the fascist Nationalist rebels, on the other hand, referred to it as *Rata* (rat). In the Soviet Union pilots affectionately called all versions of the I-16 *Ishachok* (little donkey) – for purely phonetic reasons (the nickname is derived from the Russian pronunciation of the designation, **ee**-shes**nahd**tsat').

Despite the fact that this variant was known to have been in production from 1937 to 1939, production figures have been found only for 1938 and 1939 when 274 and 53 were built respectively.

The **I-16 *tip* 6** was an interim model built in response to criticism from Soviet partici-

pants in the Spanish Civil War. They maintained that the twin machine-gun armament of the I-16 was inadequate; by comparison, the Polikarpov I-15 biplane had four machine guns. It had originally been hoped that the new ShKAS with their 1,800 rounds per minute rate of fire, compared with the 750 of the I-4's PV-1, would be satisfactory. Later experience in Spain was to prove, once and for all, the inadequacy of having only two machine guns. Andrey A. Borovkov and his colleagues worked through the night at *zavod* 21 to install a third synchronised ShKAS in the lower fuselage. After successful tests on the following day, a batch of thirty *tip* 6, as the version had been designated, was built and hastily despatched to Spain. This was seen as an emergency stop-gap measure and work started immediately on further armament additions.

Above and below: The same aircraft with a highly unusual aerial mast from which twin aerials are stretched to the fin. Bracing wires connect these to the wings.

The **I-16 *tip* 9** was the prototype of a proposed Shturmovik variant described in more detail in the 'Prototypes and Projects' section.

The **I-16 *tip* 10 (I-16 M-25V)** introduced in 1937 was the first new major sub-type of the I-16. Such was the urgency to supply them to the Spanish government during the Civil War that all improvements could not be installed at the start of production but were introduced as parts became available. The definitive version had the 750 hp (560 kW) M-25V engine and all had four 7.62 ShKAS machine-guns; two mounted above the engine and two in the wings. New, tighter regulations on aircraft structures were introduced in 1937 requiring that that of the I-16 be strengthened. Extra ribs were added to support the upper surface of the wings and the span of the ailerons was shortened. Landing speed was reduced by the installation of pneumatically operated flaps but from spring 1939 onwards these flaps became mechanically actuated. A PAK-1 reflector sight replaced the OP-1 telescopic version and a retractable ski undercarriage was developed for winter use.

An improved 'plexiglass' canopy with steel frames was installed but most aircraft had the sliding section discarded, leaving an open cockpit protected only by the fixed windscreen. Many had the OP-1 tube sight replaced by a PAK-1 reflector sight. All these changes increased the empty weight to 1,327 kg (2,926 lb.) and the flying weight to 1,716 kg (3,784 lb.). The performance figures were similar or slightly better than those of the *tip* 5 except for service ceiling and range which both showed a slight deterioration. Although this variant had been in production since 1937 it did not pass its State Acceptance Tests until February 1939. No record has been found of the number of *tip* 10s assembled at *zavod* 21 in 1937 but it is known that 508 were delivered in 1938 and 426 in 1939. Many of the surviving *tip* 10 models were converted into *tip* 18s or 24s in the last quarter of 1939.

The **I-16 *tip* 12 (I-16P, *pushechnyy*,** cannon-armed) was a 1936 development of the I-16 *tip* 5 with additional armament. Two ShVAK 20 mm cannons ([*pushka*] *Shpital'novo i Vladimirova, aviatsionnaya, kroopnokalibernaya* – Shpital'nyy & Vladimirov Heavy Aircraft Cannon) were mounted in the wing centre sections and fired outside the arc of the propeller; the two nose-mounted ShKAS synchronised machine-guns were retained. The weight increase of 100 kg (220 lb) had the inevitable result of adversely affecting its rate of climb and manoeuvrability. A small batch of twelve of this version was manufactured in 1938 for use in the Spanish Civil War.

**Three views of the prototype I-16 *tip* 10 on skis.**

Right: A production I-16 *tip* 10 on skis after nosing over on landing (here the aircraft has been lifted right side up).

Below and bottom: The prototype I-16 *tip* 12 (TsKB-12P) armed with two 20-mm ShVAK cannons and two machine guns during State acceptance trials at NII VVS. The aircraft wears an unusual red/silver colour scheme; note the early-style sliding canopy and absence of landing gear doors.

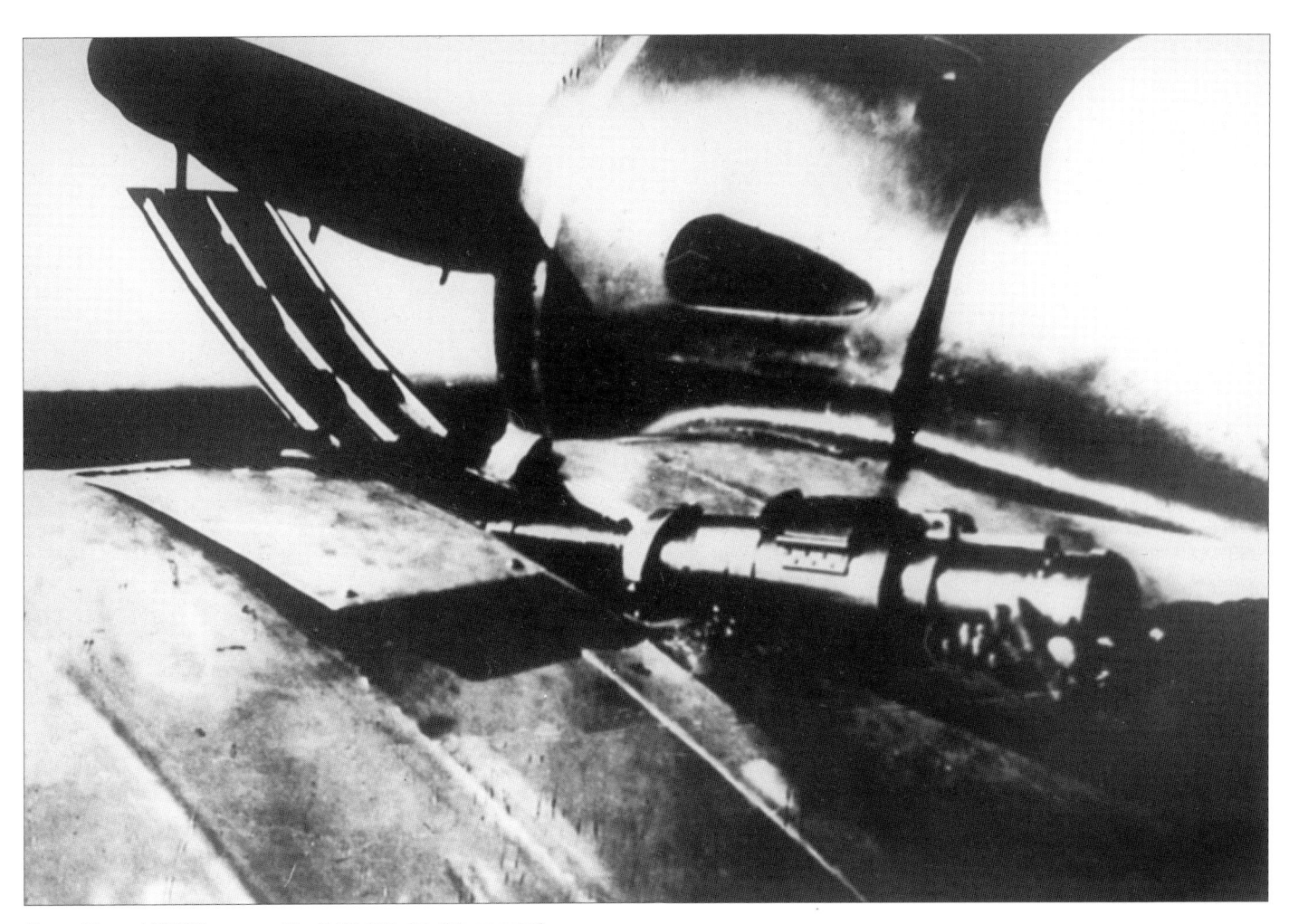

Above: The port ShVAK cannon of the TsKB-12P slid aft for removal.

Above: Armourers load 20-mm ammunition into the wing bays of the I-16 *tip* 12 prototype.

The **I-16 *tip* 17** was a more heavily armed version of the I-16 *tip* 10 and its M-25V engine was more powerful than that of the *tip* 12. In this instance two 20 mm ShVAK cannons replaced the wing mounted ShKAS machine guns and were also positioned to fire outside the arc of the propeller. No change was made to the two ShKAS machine guns in the nose. The extra weight again affected performance, but the top speed only decreased by 10 km/h (6 mph) and this was considered an acceptable exchange for tripling the firepower. Retractable ski undercarriages could be fitted when required on this type and all others of a higher *tip* number, except for *tip* 29.

Altogether 27 examples of this variant were built in 1938 and a further 314 in 1939 but many *tip* 17s were later rebuilt into *tip* 27s and 28s.

The **I-16 *tip* 18**, introduced in October 1939, had a more powerful engine, the Shvetsov M-62. Essentially an M-25V with a two-stage supercharger, improved induction system and other refinements, it produced 1,000 hp (746 kW) for take-off and 800 hp (596 kW) at 2,900 m (9,500 ft). To accommodate the new engine its mountings were strengthened and the lubrication system improved by adding an extra 12 litre oil tank but slightly reducing the size of the existing one. The oil cooler was enlarged and set a little lower, giving the impression that the base of the cowling had sagged. The carburettor pressure intake pipe was placed above the enlarged oil cooler intake. It was also necessary to reposition the cutaway on the cowling ring below and to the side. A standard VFSh (*vint fikseerovannovo shahga*) fixed-pitch propeller was fitted to the first batch but this was later replaced by the VISh-6A (*vint izmenyayemovo shahga*) and ultimately, for the last batch, by the AV-1 variable pitch propellers. Each type of airscrew had an individual spinner design. Electrical supply was delivered by a type 12A, 24 volt, battery housed between the third and fourth ribs of the centreplane and accessed through a plate on the underside. Although these changes increased the gross weight to 1,830 kg (4,034 lb), performance was improved. Top speed at sea level was now 411 km/h (255mph) and at 4,400 m (14,500 ft) was 464 km/h (288 mph); climbing to 5,000 m (16,400 ft) took only 5.2 minutes. On the debit side, landing speed had increased to 130 km/h (80 mph) and it now took 18 seconds to complete a 360° turn. In its five years of production the I-16 had, in addition to changes indicated by the *tip* numbers, been subjected to a continuous development programme to rectify its faults. In particular, strenuous efforts were directed at making the aircraft easier to fly. By the time the *tip* 18 was introduced it had become a much more stable and less 'twitchy' aeroplane. Also, the majority of its pilots had grown accustomed to the monoplane concept and were able to appreciate the I-16's strengths. 177 *tip* 18s were built in 1939 but records for 1940 show only a combined total of 760 for both *tip* 18s and 24s.

The **I-16 *tip* 19 ( I-16SN)** was the designation given to a variant of the tip 10 with a new type of 7.62 mm machine gun replacing the two wing-mounted ShKAS (the nose guns were unchanged). Called the SN after its designers Savin and Norov, the new weapon had a rate of fire of 2,800-3,000 rpm, compared with the 1,800 rpm of the ShKAS and was sanctioned for production in 1937. Three aircraft with construction numbers from 19211 to 19213 were produced at *zavod* 21. After successful factory trials carried out by Tomas P. Suzi between the 15th and 26th March 1939 a few more were built and served in the VVS with the unofficial designation I-16SN.

Another variant of the I-16SN whose formal designation – if it had one – is not known, was used in Finland during the Winter War of 1939-40. In this version the ShKAS nose guns were replaced by the Ultra ShKAS with a rate of fire of 2,400 rpm.

No production figures for any version of the I-16 *tip* 19 have been found and have presumably been included in the *tip* 10 totals.

The **I-16 *tip* 20** was an attempt to remedy the inevitable loss of range that accompanies the installation of ever more powerful engines with a limited expansion for increased fuel capacity. Maximum internal fuel capacity, in this case, was 190 kg (418 lb) and at high speed this limited range to only 480 km (300 miles). Tests were carried out between March and April 1939 with several shapes of 100 litre (22 gal.) underfuselage drop tanks, but these shifted the centre of gravity further back and exacerbated an already difficult stability problem. Underwing drop tanks were then fitted to I-16 *tip* 10 construction number 1021681, and tested throughout June and July 1939. The tanks, which passed State Acceptance Trials, were made of compressed cardboard to which a bonding agent had been added and had a capacity of 93 litres (20.5 gal.). Even when carrying these drop tanks the I-16 could still dive at an angle of 60° and perform 180° turns and the top speed fell by only 21 km/h (13 mph), with endurance being increased by one hour. 80 *tip* 10s were modified at *zavod* 39 in 1939 for possible use as escort fighters to protect Tupolev SB bombers. From January 1940 all new production models had wings modified to accept two drop tanks and every fighter was delivered with a stock of six.

The **I-16 *tip* 24** was the standard production version for 1940. Some *tip* 18s were built that year in an attempt to enable zavod 1 to achieve its production target that was threatened by the reorganisation necessary for the introduction of the new model. A new engine, the Shvetsov M-63 (an improved M-62), was installed, giving 1,100 hp (821 kW) for take-off and 900 hp (671 kW) at 4,500 m (14,800 ft). A new spinner and AV-1 propeller were used together with an R-2 constant speed regulator for the engine. Piloted by A. Nikashin, the prototype completed its State Acceptance Tests by September 1939. Maximum speed at sea level was now 440 km/h (273 mph) and 489 km/h (303 mph) at 4,800 m (15,750 ft). The climb to 5,000 m (16,400 ft) was, at 5.2 minutes, the same as for the *tip* 18 but the service ceiling was increased from 9,470 m (31,070 ft) to 10,800 m (35,500 ft). A tailwheel replaced the skid and two 93 litre (20.5 gal.) drop tanks could be carried. Further improvements were made to the main undercarriage: scissor-type legs replaced the splined type and the shock absorber stroke was increased from 36 to 96 mm (14 to 38 inches). Both sides of the cockpit cover could now be folded back into the open position and a manual engine starting handle, type 'RI', was stored in the cockpit. The prototype had a radio and a gun camera that were not installed in series production aeroplanes but could be fitted later if required. 155 *tip* 24s were built in 1939 and 19 in 1941, but 1940 records show only a total figure of 760 for both *tip* 18 and 24.

The **I-16 *tip* 27** was the designation of the *tip* 18 with the two wing-mounted ShKAS machine guns replaced by 20 mm ShVAK cannons also firing outside the arc of the propeller. It is recorded that 59 *tip* 27s were assembled in 1939 but it is impossible to differentiate between *tip* 27 and 28 in 1940 when records are limited to a combined total of 277. A further six flying replicas based on some salvaged parts of wrecked aircraft integrated with many new components were built in 1995 at former *zavod* 153 in Novosibirsk. Apart from additional equipment to satisfy current safety standards the main differences were the more modern ASh-62IR engine (as used on the Antonov An-2) and the propeller.

The **I-16 *tip* 28** was the *tip* 27 with an M-63 engine or, alternatively, it could be regarded as a *tip* 24 with 20 mm ShVAK cannons replacing the wing-mounted machine guns. In 1939 sixteen I-16 *tip* 28s were built but it is impossible to identify individual *tip* figures for 1940 when it is only known that a total of 277 *tip* 27 and 28s were delivered.

The **I-16 *tip* 29** was the final production variant of this fighter and started to emerge from the production lines in the second half of 1940. It, too, had an M-63 engine but the diameter of its propeller was now only 2.7 m (8.86 ft). The gun armament comprised two 7.62 mm ShKAS machine guns mounted on the top of the nose and a 12.7 mm BS machine gun ([*poolemyot*] *Berezina, sinkhronnyy*, Berezin's Synchronised Gun) located below the engine and between the

Above and below: The prototype I-16 *tip* 17 on skis; note the protruding muzzles of the synchronised machine guns in the cowling.

Above: A three-quarters rear view of the prototype I-16 *tip* 17, showing the machine gun fairings. on the cowling The ink stamp on the photo reading 'People's Commissariat of Aircraft Industry. Classified. Main Directorate...' etc. was invariably present on photos appended to test reports.

**Above:** The prototype I-16 *tip* 17 on wheels as originally flown; the synchronised machine guns in the nose have yet to be fitted. The undercarriage is locked down for the initial flight tests and the wheel wells are faired over to cut drag and/or stop slush from getting in.

**Above and below:** These views of the I-16 *tip* 17 illustrates how close the wing cannons were to the propeller disc. The outer projection on the starboard wing is a pitot tube, not a cannon.

An I-16 *tip* 18 during NII VVS trials.

undercarriage wells. This allowed the wing guns to be removed and replaced by underwing racks each carrying three 82 mm RS-82 unguided rockets. Strips of duralumin were positioned in appropriate places to protect the wings and ailerons when the rockets were fired. In addition to the rockets, standard drop tanks could be carried. Unfortunately the BS machine guns were not available in time and were only fitted in *tip* 29s from the middle of 1940, their place in the meantime being taken by a third ShKAS. Both the oil cooler and its air intake were moved to a position between the ports for Nos. 4 and 5 cylinders although a few I-16 *tip* 29s were built with no dedicated intake, the air entering through the cooling gills. The relocation of the oil cooler left no room for the 'RI' manual starting system which had to be omitted. With this model the undercarriage legs were shortened by 32 mm (1.3 in.) and the gap between the wells increased by 41 mm (1.6 in.) to make room for the new machine gun. Retractable ski undercarriages could not be fitted to this variant. Some aircraft left the factories complete with radios and reception was enhanced by a new mast aerial placed on the starboard side of the engine cowling. As a result of these alterations the *tip* 29 was the heaviest member of the I-16 family at 2,115 kg. (4,662 lb.). The additional weight, together with the extra drag imposed by the external load, degraded performance and the time taken to climb to 5,000 m (16,400 ft) was increased to 7.25 minutes.

Maximum speed was reduced to 429 km/h (266 mph) at 4,150 m (13,600 ft). When no external load was carried top speed at the same altitude rose to 470 km/h (292 mph). In 1940 *zavod* nos. 21 and 153 assembled 570 I-16 *tip* 29s and a further 80 in 1941.

**Two-seat I-16 variants**

The **UT-2** (*Oochebno-trenirovochnyy* [*samolyot*], trainer; not to be confused with Yakovlev's primary trainer of the same name!) was the first unarmed dual-control trainer version of the I-16. It became evident from the start that a two-seat trainer was necessary because, although talented pilots could control the fighter, lesser mortals were fatiguingly challenged by its very sensitive controls. The first example (construction number 8211) powered by an M-22 engine had its first flight in early 1935. On this prototype, and two other examples that were built, both tandem individual cockpits were enclosed and both retained a retractable undercarriage.

The **UTI-2** (*tip* 14) (*Oochebno-trenirovochnyy istrebitel'*, fighter trainer) was the version chosen for mass production. As no canopies were fitted to the cockpits the pilots had to make do with windscreens. Further money-saving measures included the omission of both oxygen equipment and engine starter but, surprisingly enough, all were built with retractable undercarriages, although whilst in service some aircraft had their undercarriage made non-retractable. State trials of the UTI-2 were passed in July 1937 but by that time this variant was no longer in production. Fifty-seven UTI-2s were built in 1935 and 1936 with a further forty or fifty in 1937. By this time production of the M-22 engine had come to an end and none was available. It was, therefore, necessary to develop another version of the trainer.

The **UTI-3** was a prototype tested by Chkalov. A UTI-2 aircraft, construction number 112111, was given an M-58 engine but in spite of good reports from the test pilot neither the engine nor the aircraft was put into production. It was deemed unnecessary to introduce yet another engine type into production when an already existing M-25 could be utilised.

The **UTI-4** (*tip* 15) succeeded the UTI-2 on the production lines of *zavod* 21. It differed from the UTI-2 in having an M-25A engine. The prototype had a retractable undercarriage, as did all series-produced aircraft; later, whilst in VVS service, some aircraft were given a fixed undercarriage. Later production aircraft were fitted with the M-25V engine (V = *vysotnyy*, high-altitude, ie., with better high-altitude performance) which had the oil cooler intake pipe on the front of the cowling. The original undercarriage with splined struts was replaced by one with torque links. An oleo-pneumatic tailskid was fitted instead of one with rubber shock absorbers. Later another modification was made to the specification by the addition of two small 35 litre fuel tanks in the centreplane. Some UTI-4s received AV-1 propellers whose pitch could be altered when on the ground and several were built in 1939 equipped for night flying training.

The **UTI-4** (*tip* 15B) was an armed variant built in 1941 at *zavod* 458 in Baku, which had been evacuated in 1941 from Rostov-on-Don. Two wing-mounted unsynchronized 12.7mm BS machine guns were installed plus two attachments under each wing; one would carry three RS rockets and the other a 50 kg (110 lb) bomb. A PBP-1A reflector gunsight and a bomb site were mounted in the forward cockpit and the unused rear cockpit was given a duralumin cover. This type was tested by the 480th AP (*aviatsionnyy polk*, Air Regiment) at Kishly, as well as the 266th AP at Shemikhan. In spite of it being proclaimed a success in January 1942 there are no records of further trainers being converted.

Russian sources differ as to the actual number of two-seat trainers built but it was certainly one of the most prolifically produced variants. Mikhail Maslov in his book *Istrebitel' I-16* (© Armada, Moscow 1997) states that the number built was 3,189 but sources at TsAGI suggested only 843. All sources agree that production was at *zavody* 153 *imeni Chkalova* in Novosibirsk and 458, located in Rostov-on-Don but evacuated to Baku in late 1941.

Above and below: The I-16 *tip* 20 prototype, a converted *tip* 10 (c/n 1021681), during trials with underwing drop tanks.

Above: A side view of the same aircraft, showing to advantage the metal skin. Note the non-standard gear doors. No, this is not a non-standard fin fillet but just something in the background – probably a lorry.

This page: The white-painted I-16 *tip* 24 prototype; note the long pointed spinner.

Above and below: Two more views of the I-16 *tip* 24 prototype.

Above: Ten 15-kg (33-lb) bombs could be carried in two rows under the fuselage of the I-16 *tip* 24.

Above: The prototype of the I-16 *tip* 29, the final production version powered by an M-63 engine and equipped with a radio, during State acceptance trials at NII VVS. Note the new abbreviated spinner and the heat-resistant panels aft of the portside exhaust stubs. The projection aft of the cockpit is a gun camera fitting.

Below: This view of the I-16 *tip* 29 shows clearly the aerial mast associated with the radio. Interestingly, there was no heat-resistant panel behind the exhaust stubs on the starboard side.

Above: This head-on view of the I-16 *tip* 29 prototype shows well the drop tanks, the triple launch rails for RS-82 unguided rockets and the muzzle of the Berezin UBS machine gun at the bottom of the cowling.

Below: Rear view of the same aircraft. Note that the aerial mast is offset and inclined to starboard. Apart from the configuration seen here, the I-16 *tip* 29 was tested at NII VVS in 'clean' configuration and with external stores but minus radio

Another view of the I-16 *tip* 29 prototype with the rocket launch rails removed.

The experimental UT-2 trainer (not to be confused with Yakovlev's aircraft of the same name!), aka I-16 No. 8211 (this was the aircraft's c/n). The enclosed cockpit is clearly visible in this view.

The prototype of the UTI-2 (I-16 *tip* 14) trainer. The smooth and rounded cowling shows clearly the aircraft had an M-22 engine.

A production M-62-powered UTI-4 (I-16 *tip* 15) on test at NII VVS makes an interesting comparison with the prototype. The new cowling and spinner are evident.

Above: The sole prototype of the UTI-3 trainer. This version was powered by the experimental M-58 engine ; note the non-standard cowling front.
Below: A side view of the UTI-3, showing the non-standard windshield of the rear cockpit which incorporated a padded headrest for the front cockpit.

**Above and below:** Three-quarters rear view and front view of the UTI-3. Note the 'UTI-3' inscription on the fin. The aircraft wears a red/silver colour scheme as sometimes applied to single-seat I-16s.

Above and below: One of the UTI-4 prototypes photographed during trials at NII VVS.

This UTI-4 tied down with whatever heavy objects were at hand was photographed in 1943. As was often the case, the spinner and gear doors have been removed, suggesting the gear has been fixed down. Note the plywood blind flying hood over the trainee's cockpit and the unusual two-tone star insignia.

Chapter 4

# Prototypes & Projects

## The I-16 in Mass Production

The **I-16 *tip* 9** was a proposed *shtoormovik* (attack aircraft) version of which only one prototype, construction number 9211, was built towards the end of 1937. An armoured cockpit was installed and a battery of six 7.62 mm ShKAS machine guns on which the pilot could depress the line of fire by 10°. The guns were housed in the centreplane at its point of junction with the outer wing panels. A fixed undercarriage with trouser fairings was fitted and between the legs six shackles were installed each of which could carry a 25 kg (55 lb.) bomb. Although the type was not produced in series, one surprising discovery emerging from the tests was the significant improvement in the aircraft's directional stability.

No designation is known for the **prototype** tested in 1935 by pilot Pyotr M. Stefanovskiy. It was a standard ***tip* 4** given a **fixed undercarriage with streamlined fairings**. It is not certain whether this was wheels or skis but the latter seems more likely as the same aircraft was later used to develop retractable skis.

Another prototype without a known designation was a proposed **fighter-bomber variant** of the 20 mm cannon-armed *tip* 12. At the beginning of 1937 an example of this marque was tested at the NII VVS with various types of underwing bomb racks. The maximum bomb load carried was 280 kg but several trials were made with two FAB-100 kg (220 lb) bombs on Der-3 attachments (the letters are an abbreviation of *derzhahtel'* – holder) and four AO-10 bombs on Der-32 attachments.

The **I-161** was a design considered by *zavod* 21 towards the end of 1935 as an alternative to the I-16 *tip* 12. It had four ShKAS machine-guns in the wings and was originally destined to be fitted with underwing bomb racks to carry four 20 kg (44 lb.) bombs but a decision was taken instead to use 20 mm cannons.

**I-161** was used again in 1937 as the designation of a lighter weight version of the I-16 projected for production in 1938. It was intended to have an M-88 engine but design work was not completed. An unexplained anomaly exists in that the designation I-161 was used twice but there is no record of an I-162!

The **I-163-1** was the first I-16 to have wing flaps. Earlier models had had ailerons that could be lowered simultaneously to act as flaps. It was similar to the *tip* 5 but the tail unit and undercarriage were also redesigned. The radio was also modified by being equipped with a mast aerial. Tests were started in April 1937 and over a thousand flights were made. As a result of these tests a decision was taken to fit flaps as standard starting with *tip* 10.

The I-16 *tip* 9 prototype (aka I-16 No. 9211), an experimental ground attack version with fixed spatted ski landing gear. The aircraft is in standard olive green camouflage with yellow trim.

The I-163 development aircraft powered by an M-25E engine. Note the modified gear doors.

An I-16 *tip* 5 fitted with an experimental aft-sliding canopy and modified windshield.

The **I-163-2** had larger flaps and an experimental oleo-pneumatic undercarriage retraction system but it was never flown.

The **I-164-1 (I-16s)** was a prototype escort fighter and the first I-16 to be given the M-25V engine. Two extra fuel tanks were fitted in the wings and it was subjected to many modifications. Trials were conducted in February 1938 with Tomas P.Suzi at the controls, and a range of 2,000 km (1,240 miles) was achieved from 500 kg (1,100 lb.) fuel. In spite of this impressive performance the decision was taken to use drop tanks.

The **I-165 (I-16bis)** also had extra fuel tanks in the wings plus a new high speed wing design with rigid skinning. Other changes included a reshaped fuselage, oil-pneumatic undercarriage retraction and a different style of engine cowling for the M-62 engine. Two examples were built but never flown because they were rejected by quality control personnel. Apparently many new parts were made without drawings and the machines were unsafe.

Above right: An I-16 captive fighter hooks up to the trapeze of a TB-3 bomber equipped with Vakhmistrov's *Zveno* system.

Right: Close-up of the attachment bars linking the I-16SPB to the mother ship; note the fuel transfer line and intercom cable attached to the fighter.

Below: Close-up of the I-16's trapeze hook. This was the fighter which hooked up to the bomber's centreline station; aircraft hooking up under the wings had a different mechanism.

47

The TsKB-29, a modified I-16 *tip* 4, attached beneath the wing of a TB-3 during trials of the SPB 'composite' dive-bomber system.

The real thing – an I-16SPB with two 250-kg (551-lb) bombs attached to a TB-3 and ready to go, the summer of 1938.

The **I-166** also had an M-25V engine and was built at the request of TsAGI with a considerably reduced gross weight of 1,383 kg (3,050 lb.). A modified NACA cowl was installed with an adjustable rear slot, circular oil radiator at the front and an exhaust gas collector. This prototype was flown by T. Suzi and designed to incorporate lessons learned in the Spanish Civil war.

The **TsKB-12P** was a prototype for the I-16 tip 12 and both were also called the I-16P. This aircraft had two 20mm ShVAK cannon in the position formerly occupied by the ShKAS machine guns in the wing centre section and the ShKAS were moved further out along the wings. When the *tip* 12 went into production the machine guns, formerly on the wings, were repositioned in the fuselage above the engine.

The **TsKB-18** was an I-16 *tip* 4 that had been modified in 1935 for the ground attack role. Armour was added to protect the pilot and was positioned underneath and to the front as well as to the rear of him. Four ShKAS machine guns were installed in the wings which were strengthened to allow a bomb load of 100 kg (220 lb) to be carried.

The **TsKB-29** and **I-16SPB** (*skorosnoy pikeeruyushchiy bombardirovshchik*, Fast Dive-Bomber) was a development of the I-16 *tip* 5. A prototype with pneumatically operated undercarriage and dive brakes, the latter replacing the inboard sections of the ailerons, was tested in May 1936. The wings were strengthened and fitted with bomb racks intended to carry two 250 kg (552 lb) bombs. Preliminary tests were carried out with 100 kg (220 lb) bombs but the increased weight prevented unassisted take-off with heavier bombs. Further trials with these bombs were therefore restricted to those in which the I-16 was carried as a *Zveno* (flight, as a tactical unit) parasite fighter-bomber. The TsKB-29 was not series-produced, but about eight I-16 *tip* 5s were modified for service with the Z-SPB composites. These aircraft had an additional oil tank in the fuselage, as the engines were run while being transported under a Tupolev TB-3; fuel was supplied from the 'mother ship'. The *Zveno* configuration used for dive bombing was an I-16SPB under each wing. As the composite's inevitable slowness made it vulnerable to enemy fighters, tactics were employed to make use of the extra available range. By flying a circuitous route to the target the I-16SPBs could be released at a safe distance from the enemy defence zone and the fighter-bombers would fly back to a base on their own. This manoeuvre had the disadvantge of limiting the target to a distance of about 400 km (250 miles).

There were many similar field conversions of all variants of the I-16, but lacking the pneumatic undercarriage retraction system, in the years following the German invasion.

Top: A TB-3 carries a bombed-up I-16SPB on a sortie.
Above: An I-16SPB heads for its target after being released by the mother ship.

The **I-16SO** (*sinkhronnyy, opytnyy*, synchronised experimental) was the designation given to an aircraft, construction number 1021332, which had its wing guns removed and two 12.7 mm BS machine-guns each with 440 rounds installed in the lower half of the nose. This necessitated a reduction in the size of the fuselage fuel tank with a compensating increase in wing tank capacity. Tests were conducted from 23rd March to 9th April 1939 and were successful in spite of unpleasant cockpit fumes, the loss of a spinner on one occasion when the guns were fired and the ingestion of uncombusted propellant into the carburettor. No doubt these difficulties were expected to be overcome because it was decided to build a trial batch for testing by the VVS. There is no record of this having been done but in 1940, when the *tip* 29 went into full production, there were not enough BS guns for even one to be fitted to each aircraft, much less two. This machine-gun was so highly esteemed by the top brass that pressure to use it was subsequently put on aviation plants and OKBs.

The **I-16PS** (*pushechnyy, sinkhronnyy* = with synchronised cannon) prototype, construction number 521570, was tested about the same time as the I-16SO. Its sole armament consisted of two 20 mm ShVAK cannon, each with 175 rounds, mounted on top of the nose directly in front of the cockpit.

The **I-16V** (*vysotnyy*, high-altitude) fighter prototypes were also developed at *zavod* 156 using the TK-1 turbosuperchargers (TK = *toorbokompressor*) which had been developed by TsIAM (*Tsentrahl'nyy instituot aviatsionnovo motorostroyeniya*, Central Institute for Aeroengine Design). They were 285 mm (11.4 in.) in diameter and mounted in a fairing on the side of the cowling between two cylinder heads. Aircraft performance was maintained up to 10,000 m (32,800 ft). The first I-16V was flown in the last half of 1938 and was an I-16 powered by an M-25A to which two TK-1s had been attached.

The experimental I-16 *tip* 10 (c/n 1021582) with an M-25V engine and twin TK-1 superchargers. The intake of the port supercharger is clearly visible.

A side view of the same aircraft. Note the large metal skin panel aft of the supercharger exhaust.

Another 'I-16 Biturbo', a converted *tip* 5 (note sliding canopy), during conversion. This aircraft has an M-62 engine and TK-1 superchargers. Note how much larger the protective metal skin panel is as compared to the I-16 *tip* 10 (part of it covers the wing root).

Close-up of the uncowled engine on the M-62-powered aircraft, showing the starboard supercharger and the twin supercharger air intakes.

**This page:** NII VVS undertook a trials programme aimed at reducing the I-16's weight. These two views show one of the development aircraft with a largely unpainted cowling and the one-piece flap fully extended.

Another lightened I-16 tested by NII VVS.

The third lightened I-16. This aircraft is completely unpainted and has abbreviated gear doors and non-standard lightened wheels.

53

The M-62-powered supercharged I-16 during trials; note the heat-resistant wing root skins.

More prototypes fitted with two TK-1s followed, the first, to an M-25V engine with an AV-1 variable-pitch propeller and later to an M-62. All these aircraft had their fuselage sides and wing centreplane upper surfaces covered in thin sheets of steel to protect them from the hot exhaust gases.

Maximum speeds of 494 km/h (307 mph) at 8,600 m (28,200ft) were achieved by the M-25V aeroplane, construction number 1021582, and over 500 km/h (310 mph) at the same altitude by another with a turbosupercharged M-62. Attempts were made to fit a pressurised cockpit to an I-16 but were unsuccessful because the extra weight of 29 kg (64 lb.) shifted the centre of gravity back to a 35% position, making the fighter virtually uncontrollable. For this reason further experiments with high-altitude versions of the I-16 were abandoned.

**Retractable skis** were tested in 1936 on two M-22 powered *tip* 4 machines, construction numbers 123904 and 123906, which had NACA cowlings with cut-outs to enable the skis to be retracted. Development work continued to perfect the mechanism which was available as an option for all I-16s built from mid-1938 (i.e. some *tip* 10s and all *tip* 17s and above except *tip* 29s). To allow the skis to retract fully, with no subsequent loss of performance over that of a wheeled undercarriage, the underside of the cowling had recesses at its junction with the wing centre section and the lower ports for the exhaust pipes of Nos. 5 and 6 cylinders were omitted.

**Armament prototypes** were tested at *zavod* 156, the TsAGI plant for experimental designs known as ZOK (*Zavod opytnykh konstrooktsiy*), to which Polikarpov and some of his team had transferred in 1937. By increasing the weight in the nose the centre of gravity was moved forward, thus improving manoeuvrability, and consequently work commenced on the effects of installing more synchronised machine guns or cannons around the engine.

**In-flight refuelling experiments** began in 1930, using a Polikarpov R-5 scout biplane with a Tupolev TB-1 as a tanker. In 1936 I-16 *tip* 4, construction number 123915, was fitted with a refuelling point on the port side within reach of the pilot who attempted to catch a trailing hose from a Tupolev TB-3 tanker. To assist the pilot in maintaining control of the aircraft during this manoeuvre the throttle lever was transferred to the top of the control column and the hose adapted to detach itself automatically when the fighter's fuel tank was full.

On 22nd June pilot Yevseyev completed two inflight refuellings but the experiments were not resumed until after the war when early jet engines restricted aircraft to even shorter ranges. Another possible reason for discontinuing the experiments was that the main task of the VVS was to operate over battlefields and there was no likelihood at that time of intercontinental bombing.

An **all-wood I-16 project** was conceived at *zavod* 163, Irkutsk, in 1942 with a view to continuing production of this fighter there. Tests were successfully carried out at SibNIA (*Seebeerskiy naoochno-issledovatel'skiy institoot aviahtsii*, Siberian Aviation Research Institute), Novosibirsk, to check the structural strength of the new wings and tail assemblies.

Conversely, by this time the NKAP (*Narodnyy komissariaht aviatsionnoy pro-myshlennosti*, People's Commissariat for the Aviation Industry) had concluded that resources would be better spent on building more modern aircraft, as this design was incapable of further development.

**Spanish modifications** carried out during the Civil War of 1936-39 included engine replacements with whatever was available and so *tip* 5 and 6 could receive the M-25V and even the M-22 (from I-15 *Chatos*). *Moscas* modified in the latter way were usually relegated to training roles. *Tip* 10s sometimes had M-25As instead of M-25Vs and twelve received contraband Wright Cyclone R-1820F-24s to improve their performance at high altitude.

Machine guns were a scarce commodity and some *Moscas* carried only two ShKAS guns. This also applied to the *Moscas* being built in Alicante for the Republicans, but the aircraft captured there and completed by the Nationalists were given four. There were tales of experiments with two 20 mm ShVAK cannons replacing the wing machine guns but there is no record of this armament being used in combat in Spain.

One or two I-16 *tip* 10s were modified for photographic reconnaissance work by the addition of a second cockpit behind the pilot.

After the war the *tip* 10s serving with the *Ejercito del Aire* (the Spanish Air Force) received flat strengthened glass windscreens. Also several of this type were converted to two-seat trainers with an enclosed canopy covering both cockpits; this variant received the local designation **I-16E**.

**Production of the I-16 fighter** started in 1934 and continued until 1941, although eighty-three of the two-seat trainer variant were not completed until 1942. A logistical nightmare ensued when factories, particularly *zavod* 21, were expected to build many different sub-types in the same year. As an example, the Gor'kiy plant manufactured a total of 2,207 I-16 aircraft in 1940 this number comprised *tip* 18s with M-62 engines, eight sub-types of the M-62 engined *tip* 24, permutating with and without drop tanks, rockets and radios (mercifully not all combinations were used) and finally the UTI-4 with the M-24V engine. Also a start was made on the *tip* 29. As if this were not enough, Polikarpov was trying unsuccessfully to arrange production of the I-180 as a successor to the I-16. However, there were other contenders for that honour and the selections depended on the result of ongoing discussions debating the relative merits of not only the I-180 but also the Pashinin I-21, the Mikoyan/Gurevich I-200 and the Lavochkin/Gorboonov/Goodkov LaGG-3. In spite of the colossal work-load the factory built more I-16s in that year than in any other. Fortunately for the sanity of the production management, by mid-year a halt had been called to this mayhem and decisions taken to build only the I-16 *tip* 29 while preparing for the production of its newly selected successor, the LaGG-3.

In Siberia, *zavod* 153, which was later to become *imeni V. P. Chkalova*, had been built and in 1937 started to produce the I-16 *tip* 5. In that year six acceptable aircraft were delivered to the VVS and by 1940 this number had built up to 503, including some trainers. Production of the I-16 ceased there in 1941 after a total of 1,301 had been built.

The third factory to make the I-16 was at Rostov-on-Don where, in 1939, the local vehicle assembly plant was transferred to the aircraft industry as *zavod* 458. This large plant turned out no fewer than 20,250 lorries in 1940 while gearing up for the UTI-4 variant for which thirty sets of parts, as well as jigs and documentation, had been received. Components were also manufactured locally; for instance, *zavod* 457 in Zaporozh'ye made undercarriages and the Uritskiy factory of Rostov-on-Don built the fuselages. Aircraft production started and the first trainer left the factory in March 1941, not long before the German invasion which forced an evacuation of the plant to Baku where the same *zavod* number was used. Here 83 UTI-2s were assembled in 1942 – the last of the I-16 variants to be built.

When the Sino-Soviet Non-Aggression Pact was signed on 21st August 1937 it contained secret clauses promising military aid to China. As a direct consequence of this an aircraft assembly plant was built in Urumchi in Western China. This plant was included in the list of Soviet defence plants as *zavod* 600. Aircraft built in the Soviet Union were first dismembered and taken by lorry to the new factory where they were re-assembled. In addition to assembly work the factory manufactured I-16 components. By mid-1941 143 examples of I-16 variants were in store there and it was decided before the German invasion to fly them to the USSR. All arrived safely in Ulan-Ude with the exception of one which crashed en route.

The above production figures (excluding the replicas built in 1995-97) are those quoted by Mikhail Maslov in his book '*Istrebitel' I-16*' published in 1997 by Armada of Moscow. Figures obtained from TsAGI gave a similar grand total of 10,293 but differ considerably in the number of two-seat trainers built, suggesting 843 against 3,189 in Maslov's book. In addition another 42 were built in Spain, 4 supplied new to the Republicans and a further 38 completed by the Nationalists.

### Annual production by factory in the USSR

| *Zavod* No. | 21 | 39 | 153 | 458 | Annual Totals |
|---|---|---|---|---|---|
| 1934 | | 50 | | | 50 |
| 1935 | 527 | 4 | | | 531 |
| 1936 | 902 | 4 | | | 906 |
| 1937 | 1,881 | | 6 | | 1,887 |
| 1938 | 1,070 | | 105 | | 1,175 |
| 1939 | 1,571 | | 264 | | 1,835 |
| 1940 | 2,207 | | 503 | | 2,710 |
| 1941 | 336 | | 423 | 356 | 1,115 |
| 1942 | | | | 83 | 83 |
| 1995 | | | 6 | | |
| *Zavod* Totals | 8,494 | 58 | 1,307 | 439 | 10,298 |

**Russian Naval Aviation had many I-16 fighters. Here is a line of them ready for take off.**

Above: Boresighting the machine guns of an I-16 *tip* 29 '75 White' operated by the 71st IAP. The aircraft wears a two-tone camouflage and has two launch rails for RS-82 rockets under each wing.
Below: A GAZ-MM truck fitted with the Hucks starter system is used to start the engine of a rocket-armed Baltic Fleet Air Arm I-16 *tip* 6 in August 1941.

Chapter 5

# Ishachok Anatomy

The technical description of the I-16 *tip* 24, the standard production variant of 1940, reflects the changes introduced into the I-16 as a result of experience gained with it in Soviet Air Force service and in the battles of the Spanish Civil War. In essence it was of mixed wood and metal construction but the metal parts were kept to a minimum, as metal was in short supply. Lacking the more complex techniques needed for all-metal aircraft, it was ideally suited to the production facilities available in the USSR and this was no doubt a reason for its continuation in production even though outclassed in performance by its contemporaries in Britain and Germany.

A short fuselage, round in cross-section, was mostly of pine, ash and plywood with steel bracing to reinforce potentially weak areas. There were eleven frames, four longerons and eight stringers. The shell covering them was made of *shpon*, a material manufactured from strips of birch wood bonded together with casein glue, with each layer positioned at right angles to its neighbour for extra strength. The shell was in two halves, split in the vertical plane and fitted around the carcass. It was secured with zinc pins and casein glue. Plywood was used to reinforce junctions, cut-out sections and mountings. Varying thicknesses of *shpon* were used: the first seven sections were 5.5 mm thick on the top half and 2.5 mm below whereas the whole of the rear sections was only 2.0 mm thick. A panel giving access to radios, if they were fitted, was located between frames 7 and 8 on the starboard side of the fuselage. After the assembly of the centreplane and fairings a smooth finish was achieved by covering any holes and crevices with a nitro-filling. All external surfaces were then coated with nitro-cellulose glue onto which calico was affixed. The fuselage was given a final filling before it was painted. By 1940 the interior surfaces of the fuselage were protected by being given a coat of AKh-9 grey enamel paint; this had superseded the use of grey oil paint.

As mentioned previously, the centreplane which carried most of the weight consisted of two stainless steel spars made into a rigid structure by connecting them with duralumin ribs and tubular struts. The joint between the fuselage and the centreplane was predominantly covered with wood but some duralumin was employed at the rear. Built into the centreplane near the joint with the outer wings were access panels for loading and servicing machine guns. The outer wing panels had a similar structure to the centreplane and were joined to it by tubular fittings with threaded ends. Although the *tip* 24 prototype had plywood skinning on the upper wing surfaces, fabric was used in production aircraft to cover the wings and this received four coats of clear lacquer followed by two coats of green paint for the top surfaces and three of light grey for the undersides which also had a coat of clear oil-based aircraft lacquer No. 17.L. Duralumin strips were used to cover the gaps between centreplane and outer wings and to reinforce the leading edges of the wings. Wing flaps were fitted along the trailing edge of the centre section and these had a maximum deflection of 60° and on this *tip* were mechanically operated. Ailerons had a duralumin structure with a slightly shorter span than the first two production variants with a gap showing between them and the wings.

Up to June 1941 the finished painting of I-16s was carried out after their test flights and usually consisted of the standard regulation dark green upper surfaces and light blue undersurfaces. Some, however, following a joint decision by GUAP and VIAM in the

**Above:** The sliding canopy and OP-1 gunsight of the I-16 *tip* 4/*tip* 5.
**Below:** Close-up of the windscreen and PAK-1 collimator gunsight of the I-16 *tip* 24.

Above: The starboard wingtip and tail unit of an I-16 *tip* 29. The metal framework of the fin shows clearly through the fabric skin.

Below: The wheeled undercarriage of a late-production I-16; note the retraction cables running from the wheel hubs to a drum in the fuselage via the wheel wells.

Bottom: For winter operations most versions of the I-16 could be equipped with retractable skis. Note the recesses in the lower portion of the engine cowling accommodating the front ends of the skis.

summer of 1937, were painted an overall matt silver. This decision had not been fully implemented by June 1941 when the aircraft were camouflaged. No doubt the factories had carried a large stock of dark green and light blue paint! The new camouflage finish had small patches of black and green but this had hardly been applied when the Germans invaded.

National markings of five-pointed red stars, sometimes with black outlines, were painted on the sides of the fuselage and the upper and lower wings. After June 1941 stars were added to the tail fin but omitted from the underside of the wings.

To increase the operating range, piping was now fitted to enable underwing fuel tanks each of 93 litres (20.5 gals) to be utilised; they were made of compressed cardboard treated with a bonding agent. Although the drop tanks reduced the maximum speed by 21 km/h (13 mph), endurance was increased by 60 minutes. Manoeuvrability was also adversely affected in that the maximum angle of dive dropped to 60°, but 180° turns could still be performed. Factories delivered six drop tanks with each newly built fighter. Main fuel tanks in the fuselage were made of metal for aircraft built before mid-1939 but ensuing models were fitted with self-sealing tanks usually constructed by bonding a 6 mm layer of leather to a thin (0.5 mm) layer of vulcanised rubber outside of which was a steel mesh case itself covered with another layer of rubber this time 2.5 mm thick.

Both vertical and horizontal tails had a duralumin structure with fabric covering and the fin was offset 2° to port to compensate for the engine's torque. Adjustments of + or -3° could be made to the tailplane whilst the aircraft was on the ground by removing a duralumin plate; a measure which enabled mechanics to find a setting to minimise control stick loads when the centre of gravity of the aircraft was changed.

Larger 700 x 150 mm wheels were now fitted to the oleo-pneumatic shock absorbers on a three-rod pyramid strut structure and had mechanical brakes operated by a foot pedal. A longer stroke of 96 mm compared with 36mm was utilised for the shock absorbers. The undercarriage retracted inwards into the wing centre section, an operation manually executed by winding a crank through forty-four revolutions. Celluloid covered cut-outs in the cockpit floor enabled the pilot to check whether the undercarriage was retracted. The tailskid of earlier models was replaced by a damped tailwheel of 150 mm diameter which could be substituted by a tailski for snow conditions. To allow the use of retractable skis to replace the main undercarriage, recesses were provided in the underside of the fuselage; these were covered by fairings in the summer.

Accommodation for the pilot in the open cockpit was adequate but less comfortable in winter when extra thick fur-lined flying clothes had to be worn. The duralumin seat had a recess to accommodate the parachute and the back of the seat protective armour 8 mm thick weighing 30 kg (66 lb). Seat height could be adjusted through 11 cm. by the use of a handle on the right hand side. The forward view was terrible, worse even than the Bf 109, the standard by which the diabolical was measured. Two small doors aided entering and leaving the cockpit and these were sometimes opened in flight to obtain a better view. Covers on each side of the cockpit were of plexiglass mounted in steel frames which could be folded back on both sides. The gun sight was a PAK-1 reflector type. Set into the sides of the black painted instrument panel were cocking handles for the two machine-guns synchronised to fire through the propeller. Two bulbs located under the gunsight provided illumination for the panel. Flaps were actuated by a lever to the left of the seat and the undercarriage handle was to the right. Wheelbrakes were applied by a foot pedal. In comparison with contemporary Western fighters the main surprises were the lack of trimmers and artificial horizon and also it was necessary to use a bank of switches to turn on systems and instruments that needed electric power.

The gun armament of the I-16 *tip* 24 was its greatest weakness; whilst British fighters in production had eight machine guns and German fighters carried cannons, the *tip* 24 had only four 7.62 mm ShKAS machine-guns: two on the top of the nose firing through the propeller and two with 900 rounds each in the wing centre section firing just outside of the propeller's arc. However, this variant was able to carry a cluster of three RS-82 rockets under each wing just outboard of the drop tanks.

By fitting the Shvetsov M-63 engine which gave 930 hp (694kW) at 4,780 m. (15,700 ft) the *tip* 24 was the fastest production variant and had a top speed 489 km/h (303 mph); later models with the same engine were all heavier. It also had the best rate of climb at 5.2 minutes to 5,000 m (16,400 ft) and the highest service ceiling of 10,800 m. (35,500 ft).

The engine cowling consisted of a front ring, of diameter 1388 mm (54.6 inches behind which were 6 removable panels attached and clasped around the fuselage with rods and clips. Air entered the engine through nine wedge shaped apertures arranged around the spinner in the cowling, in the front ring. After cooling the engine hot air exited through eight apertures in the panels which also accommodated the individual exhaust pipes. Behind this arrangement was a stainless steel ring 0.5 m (20 inches) wide closing the gap between cowling and the wing leading edge.

AV-1 two blade propellers were fitted with a spinner of 530 mm (21.2 inches) diameter together with an R-2 constant rpm regulator. Set in the middle of the spinner was a socket for a Hucks starter and carried in the cockpit was an RI crank handle operated from a dedicated aperture on the right-hand side of the front fuselage in times of emergency.

A 100-kg (220-lb) FAB-100 bomb on the centreline bomb cradle of an I-16 *tip* 24.

## Data for the I-16 variants

|  | Tip 4 | Tip 5 | Tip 10 | Tip 15 (UTI-4) |
| --- | --- | --- | --- | --- |
| Engine | M-22 | M-25A | M-25V | M-25A |
| Span | 9.0 m (29.5 ft) | 9.0 m (29.5 ft) | 9.0 m (29.5 ft) | 9.0 m (29.5 ft) |
| Length | 5.9 m (19.2 ft) | 6.0 m (19.7 ft) | 6.1 m (19.9 ft) | 6.0 m (19.7 ft) |
| Wing area | 14.54 m$^2$ (157 sq. ft) | 14.54 m$^2$ (157 ft$^2$) | 14.54 m$^2$ (157 ft$^2$) | 14.54 m$^2$ (157 ft$^2$) |
| Weight empty | n.a. | 1,118 kg (2,471 lb) | 1,327 kg (2,933 lb) | 1,156 kg (2,555 lb) |
| Weight loaded | 1,354 kg.(2,992 lb.) | 1,508 kg (3,333 lb) | 1,716 kg (3,792 lb) | 1,458 kg (3,222 lb) |
| Max. speed at sea level | 362 km/h (224 mph) | 390 km/h (242 mph) | 398 km/h (247 mph) | 398 km/h (247 mph) |
| Max. speed at altitude | 346 km/h (215 mph) 3,000 m (9,800 ft) | 445 km/h (276 mph) 3,000 m (9,800 ft) | 448 km/h (278 mph) 3,000 m (9,800 ft) | 450 km/h (279 mph) 3,000 m (9,800 ft) |
| Climb to 5,000 m | 9.9 mins | 7.3 mins | 6.9 mins | 6.4 mins |
| Service ceiling | 7,440 m (24,400 ft) | 9,100 m (29,800 ft) | 8,500 m (27,800 ft) | 9,000 m (29,500 ft) |
| Range | 680 km (420 miles) | 540 m (335 miles) | 525 km (326 miles) | 364 km (226 miles) |
| Time for 360° turn | 12-14 secs | 14-15 secs | 16-18 secs | 16-18 secs |
| Take off run | n.a. | 220 m (720 ft) | 260 m (850 ft) | 248 m (810 ft) |
| Landing run | n.a. | 200m (660 ft) | 288 m (940 ft) | 278 m (910 ft) |

The starboard ShVAK cannon of an I-16 *tip* 17.

## Data for the I-16 variants (continued)

|  | *Tip* 18 | *Tip* 24 | *Tip* 28 | *Tip* 29 |
|---|---|---|---|---|
| Engine | M-62 | M-63 | M-63 | M-63 |
| Span | 9.0 m (29.5 ft) | 9.0 m (29.5 ft) | 9.0 m (29.5 ft) | 9.0 m (29.5 ft) |
| Length | 6.0 m (19.9 ft) | 6.1 m (20.1 ft) | 6.1 m (20.1 ft) | 6.1 m (20.1 ft) |
| Wing area | 14.54 m$^2$ (157 ft$^2$) | 14.54 m$^2$ (157 ft$^2$) | 14.54 m$^2$ (157 ft$^2$) | 14.54 m$^2$ (157 ft$^2$) |
| Weight empty | 1,433 kg (3,167 lb) | 1,382 kg. (3,054 lb) | 1,403 kg. (3,111 lb) | 1,545 kg* (3,414 lb) |
| Weight loaded | 1,830 kg. (4,044 lb.) | 1,882 kg (4,159 lb) | 1,988 kg (4,393 lb) | 1,966 kg* (4,344 lb) |
| Max. speed sea level | 413 km/h (256 mph) | 410 km/h (254 mph) | 427 km/h (265 mph) | 419 km/h (260 mph) |
| Max. speed at altitude | 461 km/h (286 mph) 4,400 m (14,400 ft) | 489 km/h (303 mph) 4,850 m (15,750 ft) | 463 km/h (287 mph) 2,000 m (6,600 ft) | 470 km/h (291 mph) 5,500 m (18,000 ft) |
| Climb to 5,000 m | 5.4 mins | 5.2 mins | 5.6 mins | 5.8 mins |
| Service Ceiling | 9,300 m (30,500 ft) | 10,800 m (35,500 ft) | 9,900 m (32,500 ft) | 9,800 m (32,100 ft) |
| Range | 485 km (300 miles) | 440 m (270 miles) | n.a. | 440 km (270 miles) |
| Time for 360° turn | 17 secs | 17-18 secs | 17-19 secs | 16-17 secs |
| Take off Run | 210 m (690 ft) | 260 m (850 ft) | 210 m (690 ft) | n.a. |
| Landing Run | 210 m (690 ft) | 300 m (980 ft) | 240 m (790 ft) | n.a. |

* Some *tip* 29s carried extra equipment, such as radios and drop tanks, bringing their loaded weight up to 2,115 kg (4,662 lb) and their performance was degraded.

Chapter 6

# The I-16 in Action

The operational history of the I-16 was long and varied. First examples of the *tip* 4 from the production lines of *zavody* 21 and 39 came into operation with the VVS from late 1934. They were used for general training and particularly to acclimatise fighter pilots, not only to a monoplane with a retractable undercarriage and enclosed cockpit but also to an aeroplane which was difficult to fly, unforgiving to the clumsy but very rewarding to the skilful. The first 'standard' service version, the *tip* 5 had not been operational in the VVS for very long when 31 were despatched by boat to Spain in October 1936 to aid the government – Republican side, struggling against the fascist, so-called Nationalist, rebellion which was supported by Germany and Italy.

Not only aircraft but also ground staff and pilots from the 3rd *eskadril'ya* (squadron) of the 1st **aviabrigada** at Bryansk joined the Republicans. Two *Mosca escuadrillas* were created as part of *Grupo* 12 into which all Soviet-built aircraft had been administratively collected and formed part of the defences of Madrid. It was over this city that they had their baptism of fire on 9th November 1936. Initially based at Alcala de Henares, they made a major contribution by forcing the Germans to stop using Junkers Ju 52/3m's as bombers during daylight. On the 15th November *Moscas* (Flies), as the I-16s were known to the Republicans, shot down two Fiat C.R.32s without loss of any aircraft themselves until they engaged the Fiat biplanes in close combat. This error of judgement cost them three I-16s, as the Italian-built aeroplanes were extremely manoeuvrable and their armament of two 12.7 mm machine guns far more effective than the two 7.62 guns carried by the Russian aircraft. Drastic measures were called for to put an end to this situation and, utilising their aircraft's excellent rate of climb the Russian pilots adopted the ruse of executing fast passing movements through the Nationalists' formations attacking from above or below the enemy at will. So successful were these tactics they lost only two more *Moscas* in the next fourteen weeks. The fascist fighter squadrons were also using Heinkel He 51s and the pilots of both types of biplanes were instructed not to attack I-16s unless they had numerical ascendancy. Another result of the apparent superiority of the *Mosca* was that the Germans were forced to rush the Messerschmitt Bf 109 into action in mid-1937 which was more quickly than they would have liked, but in spite of this it still proved to be a very effective fighter.

Outside Spain the press referred to the I-16s as 'Boeings' in the mistaken belief that

**ALARM! HOT SCRAMBLE!!!** Ground crews remove fir branches used to camouflage two I-16s (a *tip* 10, in the foreground, and a *tip* 17) during a practice alert in 1938.

Two views of 9 Black, a Spanish Republican Air Force (*Fuerza Aerea Republicana*)/1ª *Escuadrilla de Moscas* I-16 *tip* 5. Note battle damage to the starboard mainwheel and the missing machine guns.

Two views of an I-16 *tip* 10 captured by the Nationalists. The domino piece on the tail is a squadron badge, a leftover from its days with the Republican Air Force.

they were a version of that company's P-26 built under licence in Russia. This error was caused by their arrogance in not believing that the Soviets could develop outstanding aircraft, or anything else for that matter, a mistake that was repeated many times by the Germans to their cost during the Second World War. Strangely enough, two American pilots, Frank Tinker and Harold Dahl, who flew fighters for the Republicans in Spain endorsed this view of the I-16's origin, and an article in *The New York Times* of 21st April 1937 was headed *War Shows Lead of US Airplanes*.

A second batch of thirty-one I-16 *tip* 5s arrived at Cartagena around the end of the year, followed some weeks later by a further thirty-one fighters and four UTI-4 trainers. Accompanying these aircraft were staff of the 142nd *Aviabrigada* of Bobruisk and sixty Spanish pilots who had learned to fly the I-16 at Kirovograd.

By this time the exclusively *Moscas Grupo* 21 had been formed with the 3rd *Escuadrilla* at Albacete in February 1937 and a 4th *Escuadrilla*, based at Escatron, was added in July. Ivan Kopets, alias 'Jose', was the first group commander and he was succeeded by Yevgeniy Ptookhin.

A fourth consignment of thirty-one I-16s docked on 10th August 1937 and the 5th and 6th *Escuadrillas* formed in October at Liria Reus and Cabeza de Buey respectively. On the 15th October five squadrons of *Moscas* and two of *Chatos* attacked the airfield at Garapinillos near Zaragoza; the 4th *Escuadrilla* was not present as it was already occupied with fighting in the Northern Zone. Three Ju 52/3m's, two Heinkel He 46s and six C.R.32s were destroyed and about twenty other aircraft damaged.

The next delivery took place in March 1938 when thirty-one more *Moscas* arrived to

**Above:** C.8-41, an all-silver I-16 *tip* 10 *Super Mosca* in post-war Spanish Air Force markings operated by the Moron Fighter School.

**A squadron of Spanish Nationalist Air Force (*Ejercito del Aire*) I-16s. All the aircraft have white cowlings and tails.**

A line-up of Chinese-built late-model UTI-4s (Chung-28As). The second aircraft in the row carries the tactical code '31 Yellow'.

be followed in June and July by further deliveries which are believed to have numbered at least ninety. Unfortunately, incomplete records provide no proof of the actual number delivered. The highest serial number noted, but not photographed, was CM-276 which gives an indication, but no proof, that a maximum of 276 fighters were received. Deliveries recorded in this article total 245 fighters and it seems reasonable to assume that the actual number received by the Republicans from the USSR was somewhere between 245 and 276.

These reinforcements allowed the formation of the 7th and last *Escuadrilla de Moscas* at Pachs. Deliveries in 1938 were all of *tip* 10. Russian sources state 455 fighters and 20 trainers were despatched but three ships were sunk and a total of 96 ships carrying military cargo, not all of them aircraft, were detained in neutral ports. Insufficient records have been preserved to allow historians to reconcile the difference between the numbers despatched and those received.

In addition to their genuine desire to help their allies, both the Soviet and German authorities were equally keen on testing the effectiveness of their latest weapons in the hot and dusty conditions found in Spain. The I-16 undercarriage wheels were found to be too narrow for the bumpy Spanish airfields and were increased in size from 750x100 mm to 750x150 mm; undersides of the tail unit were damaged by stones thrown up while taxiing, a problem solved by the addition of two layers of protective fabric; and cockpit canopies crazed even more quickly than in the USSR so that pilots usually flew with them permanently fixed open. A further problem of the dust being ingested by the air-cooled engines was solved by fitting oil coolers and carburettor intake filters. Much more intractable to a 'quick fix' was the inadequate armament of just two 7.62 mm ShKAS machine guns, and a solution to this had to be sought at *zavod* 21 in Gor'kiy. As already recounted, in the course of one night Borovkov and his team fitted a synchronised ShKAS in the nose beneath the engine and the following day this was tested and approved. Very shortly afterwards a batch of thirty of this variant, called I-16 *tip* 6, was built and shipped to Spain.

A more effective solution was incorporated into the next series production variant the I-16 *tip* 10 by equipping it with two synchronised ShKAS machine-guns installed above the engine to supplement its two wing guns. As a result of this and many other improvements this version was known in Spain as the *Super Mosca*, sometimes abbreviated to Super.

Up to May 1937 all the pilots of *Moscas* had been Soviet volunteers and they served with distinction in the Battles of Guadalajara, Huesca, La Granja and La Jarama. Together with the *Chato escuadrillas* their presence and victories in the skies over Madrid raised the morale of the defending Republican troops, making a major contribution to the successful defence of the city in 1937. Spanish pilots and pilots of other nationalities then began to join the *Mosca* units and by December 1937 *Grupo* 21 had a Spanish commander, Manuel Aguirre. Soviet pilots were gradually replaced and all had returned home by the end of November 1938. The commanders of the *Mosca escuadrilla* changed frequently and there is no consensus among historians as to names and dates; therefore the confusing subject will not broached in this book.

Two expeditions were mounted to send fighters to the aid of the besieged Republicans in the northern enclave where they fought valiantly against overwhelming odds until the Nationalists prevailed there in October 1937. Reports of three or four *Moscas* attacking enemy formations of seventy aircraft were commonplace and at the end of this campaign only one *Mosca*, piloted by Luis de Frutos, was left to escape to France.

In the meantime, battles continued to rage in the south and in July 1937, *Moscas* clashed with the Bf 109B. To begin with they were evenly matched but it was not long before the German pilots recognised the superiority of their aircraft above 3,000 m (9,800 ft) and took up positions high above the Soviet aircraft either to lure them upwards into battle on uneven terms or to give themselves the advantage of a diving attack. Although these tactics did not produce total air supremacy, the attrition of I-16s was considerable.

To improve their high-altitude performance twenty-four Wright Cyclone R-1820F-24 engines were smuggled out of the USA and by September 1938 had been fitted to twelve I-16 *tip* 10 *Super Moscas* of the 4th *Escuadrilla*. These enabled the Republican pilots to turn the tables on the Messerschmitt pilots who, although operating at 6,000 m (20,000 ft), found themselves attacked from above by fighters with superior manoeuvrability. Problems had occurred with the machine guns freezing up at high altitude but these had been resolved when J-A. Lopez Smith designed a device that diverted hot filtered engine exhaust gases over the guns'

mechanisms. As a result of their ability to operate successfully at high altitudes and their white propeller bosses, the 4th *Escuadrilla* was nicknamed *Nariz fria* (Cold nose), and 4th *Escuadrilla* pilots were dubbed *Chapete* (Baby's dummy) because of their oxygen masks.

An example of one of their successes took place on 18th September when twelve modified *Super Moscas* 'jumped' sixteen Bf 109s and shot down four. The melee escalated with the arrival of *Chatos* and other standard *Moscas,* after which seven more Messerschmitts were destroyed. Republican losses in this encounter were not recorded. As the rebels captured more and more territory I-16s were used in the ground attack role, with a corresponding increase in the number of *Moscas* lost. Attrition of aircraft, spares and pilots accelerated as the number of Nationalist fighters increased. By this time losses had mounted in battles around Teruel and fighting now continued on the Ebro where huge air battles involving up to 200 participants were taking place.

Realising that supplies of aircraft from the USSR succeeded in only a short-term solution to their lack of fighters, the Republican

government signed a licensing agreement with the USSR to enable them to build I-15 *Chato* biplanes in Spain. Understandably the Spanish, not content with the obsolescent design offered to them, decided to manufacture the I-16 *tip* 10 illegally and, after making drawings from aircraft and parts supplied by the USSR, State Aircraft Factory No. 15 in Alicante during the summer of 1938 prepared to manufacture 1,000 I-16 *tip* 10s. By the end of the year four aircraft had been completed and delivered to the front but a shortage of guns resulted in the fitting of only two wing guns. These aircraft were serialled CH-001 to CH-004. Soviet-built aeroplanes initially received identification numbers consisting of two or three digits but this was later rationalised and survivors received serials in the CM-XXX series. Trainers, either UTI-4s or I-16s, did not have any individual aircraft marks visible on them.

Between September 1937 and November 1938 the number of airworthy I-16s stabilised at approximately forty to fifty and as the establishment of a fighter escuadrilla required twelve aircraft most of them would be understrength. From November 1938 the number of serviceable I-16s plummeted until only seven

**Finnish Army soldiers inspect an I-16 (64 Red) which was damaged in combat and stood on its nose during the subsequent forced landing in deep snow. The aircraft is fitted with four missile rails.**

survived destruction or capture to escape to France when Republican resistance collapsed in March 1939.

By the end of the war twelve well-used *Moscas* had been captured by the Nationalists and they found a further ten completed at the Alicante factory. These twenty-two aeroplanes formed *Grupo* I-W; aircraft were numbered in the series IW-1 to IW-22 which were displayed on the aircraft in black except for the squadron commanders who had white numbers. A further thirty-five incomplete airframes were transferred to a converted sherry bodega in Jerez de la Frontera for completion and of these, twenty-eight had been delivered by the end of 1941 to the *Ejercito del Aire*. By this time the *Moscas*, renamed *Ratas* (Rats) from their Nationalist *nom de guerre*, had been given the type designation C8 and aircraft painted with identification numbers starting C8-1.

China was the next country where the I-16 was in action. Military aid to China was guaranteed in the secret clauses of the Sino-Soviet Non-Aggression Pact of 1937. At first this aid consisted only of aircraft and non-combatants such as flying instructors and engineers. In the two years commencing October 1937, 885 aircraft of all types, including 216 I-16 *tip* 5s and 10s, were sent to China and, as mentioned earlier, a factory built in Urumchi to assemble and manufacture some I-16 parts. The lack of training of Chinese pilots, who referred to the I-16s as 'Swallows', led to the loss of large numbers of aircraft both in accidents and combat.

Four *eskadril'yi* of I-15*bis*'s staffed by Soviet 'volunteers' were sent in November 1937 to the Nanking area to fight in the Second Sino-Japanese War. As a result of the Japanese introducing their Mitsubishi A5M2a monoplanes (code-named *Claude* by the allies in the Second World War) two squadrons of I-15*bis*'s were replaced with the same number of I-16s in January 1938.

In their first taste of battle on 21st November three Japanese aircraft were claimed to have been destroyed without any losses to the seven I-16s involved. Many air battles took place in November and December, with the Soviets claiming air superiority. In those days the Chinese government offered cash rewards for each Japanese aircraft destroyed – and, in contrast to other nationalities serving in the Chinese Air Force, these rewards were not accepted by the Soviet pilots.

More I-16s arrived in China later in 1938 and after the fall of Nanking, with the subsequent massacres of civilians, air battles intensified. To celebrate the Emperor's birthday on 19th April fifty-four Japanese aircraft raided Wuhan and, after being intercepted by Soviet-flown I-16s and I-15*bis*'s, twenty-one failed to return. Another large air battle took place on the 31st May when 14 Japanese aircraft were lost. In March 1938 the Japanese government tried unsuccessfully to exert diplomatic pressure to persuade the USSR to withdraw from China.

Meanwhile trouble was brewing on the Mongolian border with Japanese-occupied Manchuria, now the puppet state of Manchukuo. The border was ill-defined and the Japanese had been aggressively probing into Mongolian territory along the Khalkhin-Gol river since 1936. By May 1939 this had escalated into an undeclared war when the Japanese were seen to be preparing for an attack outflanking the defences of Mongolia and its Soviet allies. Air warfare started modestly with the Soviets employing one regiment equipped with the I-15*bis* biplane and the 22nd IAP (*istre**bit**el'nyy aviatsi**on**nyy polk*, fighter aviation regiment) with I-16 *tip* 5 fighters. Opposing the Soviet fighters was the Nakajima Ki-27 (Abdul) Army Type 97 Fighter monoplane. In the first four weeks of air battles the Soviets admitted to losing four aircraft for every Japanese aircraft destroyed, a situation which resulted in the arrival on 29th May of the VVS Commander-in-Chief Yakov V. Smooshkevich to personally reorganise the allied Air Forces. He was accompanied by 21 pilots with experience in Spain and China, of whom no less than eleven were Heroes of the Soviet Union. Stalin was obviously not underestimating the importance of this conflict.

While both sides continued to build up their air and ground forces, massive air battles involving over a hundred aircraft continued to rage and on 5th June General (later Marshal) Gheorgiy K. Zhookov arrived to act as Supreme Commander. Like all other successful commanders before and since, he demanded and received substantial reinforcements. By the end of May 76 I-16s had arrived and by the end of the conflict 311 had been deployed. Later deliveries were mainly *tip* 10s and 17s and, although some *tip* 18s were in time for the 'war', most arrived after it had ended. A large air battle took place on the 22nd June 1939 and involved 120 Japanese aircraft and 95 Soviet fighters. After two and a half hours 31 Japanese aircraft fell for the loss of 11 Soviet. Battles on this scale were not uncommon.

Five I-16s fitted with RS-82 unguided rocket launchers under their wings attacked a force of Japanese bombers escorted by Ki-27 fighters. A volley of the rockets, which had proximity fuses, was launched at the close formation of enemy fighters. Fortune this time favoured the brave and after two Japanese aircraft had been destroyed the rest promptly returned to base. This new weapon was extensively tested and claimed, in all, 13 aircraft.

Both sides in this conflict wildly exaggerated their successes. For example, the Japanese at the time claimed to have destroyed a total of 1,260 aircraft which was two and a half times as many as the Soviets actually deployed! For their part the Soviets were more modest in claiming 645 when only 500 were pitted against them.

In the land battles, General G. Zhookov was victorious, claiming to have incapacitated 61,000 Japanese troops for the loss of 11,000 Soviet dead. The 'war' ended on 16th September 1939 when the Japanese withdrew behind the Manchukuo border. By acting decisively and ruthlessly when provoked by the Japanese the USSR won more than a tactical victory, for it is no exaggeration to say that it later allowed the withdrawal of large armies from the East to reinforce the defence of Moscow and Stalingrad and mount counter-attacks against the Germans. These were the very same reinforcements that Hitler repeatedly told his generals did not exist! Stalin mounted these offensives because he confidently believed that as a result of the Khalkhin-Gol conflict the Japanese would not attack the USSR.

The I-16 played its part in this victory. In skilful hands it proved to be more than a match for the Type 97 fighter. It was slightly less agile than its opponent but a little faster on the level and had a better rate of climb.

The invasion of Poland by the USSR on 17th September 1939 was a direct result of the secret clauses in the Soviet-German Non-Aggression Pact of 1939 in which the USSR was allowed by the Third Reich to annexe Eastern Poland in return for accepting German domination over the rest of that country. Although this took the form of a full-scale military attack, little or no resistance was offered as the Polish armed forces were fully occupied fighting the Germans. Several regiments of I-16s took part but there are no records of any air battles.

The Winter War with Finland started on 30th November 1939 when Soviet troops invaded their neighbour. Little is recorded about the details of the air war except for Finnish claims of having destroyed 207 Russian aircraft for the loss of 48 of their own. At that time the I-16 was the most important fighter in the Soviet inventory and played an important, if unrecorded, part in the war which was fought in the depths of winter. It must have been acutely uncomfortable to fly with an open cockpit and the cranking up of the undercarriage almost impossible. In those conditions the skis would have replaced the wheeled undercarriage, but even so the frost and snow must have made taking off and landing even more hazardous. One innovation that was tested and used in this war was the carrying of underwing drop tanks – a development covered earlier in this book under I-16 *tip* 20. As other air forces were later to learn to their cost,

VH-201, the first captured I-16 to be flown by the *Ilmavoimat* (Finnish Air Force). The VH serial prefix denotes 'vihollisen havittaja' (enemy fighter). The aircraft was operated by LeLv 30 (30th Air Squadron).

UT-1, a captured UTI-4 operated by TLeLv 35.

This page: Many I-16s and other VVS RKKA aircraft were destroyed or damaged on the ground by the *Luftwaffe* in the first hours of the Great Patriotic War before they had a chance to engage the enemy.

Above: 1-W-30, a captured I-16 *tip* 10 operated by *Grupo* 26 in 1944-45.

This page and opposite page, below: 1-W-1, the first I-16 to be operated by the Nationalists (a *tip* 5). Captured in damaged condition in 1939 and rebuilt, the aircraft was flown by *Grupo* 1W based at Madrid-Cuatro Vientos. Note how the aircraft's colour scheme changed with time.

1-W-6/161, a captured *tip* 10, in sand/brown mottled camouflage. The aircraft was operated by the Moron Fighter School in 1940-41.

This I-16 was flown by the Republican Air Force's 4ª *Escuadrilla de Moscas* prior to capture by the Nationalists.

Another captured example with the Moron Fighter School badge on the fuselage.

Two Nationalist I-16 *tip* 10s hangared for maintenance. The far aircraft has a 'Yoke and arrows' emblem on the fuselage roundel.

Left: This I-16 *tip* 5 was probably thrown on its nose by the blast wave of a bomb exploding behind it; note shrapnel damage to the wings and tail.

Below: This I-16 *tip* 5 was captured intact by advancing *Wehrmacht* troops at Siauliai, Lithuania.

Above: 4 Red, another *tip* 5 captured at Riga in near-perfect condition along with several other aircraft; the MiG-3 fighter and SB-2M-103 bomber visible in the background are distinctly the worse for wear.

An I-16 fighting on the North-Western Front pictured during overhaul in November 1942, with an Il'yushin IL-2 attack aircraft in the background. Both aircraft wear freshly-applied winter camouflage.

bombers operating in daylight need escort fighters if they are to avoid unacceptably high losses. Fortunately for both sides the war was short and ended on 13th March 1940 when Finland yielded territory to allow Leningrad to be defended more easily in the event of a German invasion.

The Finnish Air Force, always short of aircraft, took on charge three I-16s that had been captured either in the Winter War or the Extension War that flared up after the German invasion of the USSR in June 1941. Two were fighters of unknown *tip* and these were given serial numbers IR-21 and IR-101 but little is known of their function. The third aircraft, a UTI-4 trainer, was used by *Taydennyslentolaivue* 35 at Vesivehmaa for three or four months in 1942 before being withdrawn from service and stored. Here it languished until taking its place as an exhibit in the *Suomen Ilmailumuseo* (Finnish Aviation Museum) at Vantaa Airport, Helsinki. It now carries the serial number UT-1 but earlier it had been VH-22.

When the Great Patriotic War was provoked by the German invasion of Russia on 22nd June 1941 the I-16 represented 38% of all the 4,226 fighters in the five military districts (M.D.) close to the western frontier. 396 of these were in the Leningrad M.D., 142 in the Baltic, 455 in the Kiev, 143 in the Odessa and 451 in the Western Districts; in all 57 IAPs were equipped with the I-16 although some regiments had a mixture of the monoplanes and I-153 biplanes. In addition the Soviet Naval Air Force had 180 I-16s with the Baltic Fleet and 148 with the Black Sea Fleet. Facing the invaders were 1,915 I-16s, not counting the two-seat trainers. These figures clearly show that the obsolescent I-16 was the primary fighter used to defend the USSR in the opening stages of the war.

Up to the time of the invasion Stalin, in spite of being forewarned, did not believe the Germans would attack the USSR and had ordered his forces to do nothing that could be considered provocative. As a result many aircraft were left grouped openly on their airfields, providing easy targets to the invaders who struck in the early hours of 22nd June 1941. Bombs and artillery shells wreaked havoc on sixty six airfields and by sundown of the first day 1,200 Soviet aircraft had been destroyed; the Western Military District alone lost 528 on the ground and a further 210 in air combat. Surrounded by confusion and carnage, incensed Soviet pilots attacked the invaders with such fury and bravery that by the end of the first day the Germans had lost 300 aircraft.

There were many examples of the heroism of these I-16 pilots some of whom, either in desperation at having no ammunition or fired by bitter hatred, rammed enemy aircraft. Lt Koklyak of the 67th IAP shot down four of the invaders and lost his life when he rammed an Italian Savoia Marchetti SM 79. Pilots who were known to have made a successful ramming attack were made 'Heroes of the Soviet Union' but unfortunately the awards were usually posthumous. On the first day alone fifteen Soviet pilots were known to have made such ramming attacks.

A tragic story concerns the 122nd IAP which successfully took off from their Karolin air base to engage their attackers, shooting down four Dornier Do17Z bombers. Together with the rest of their division, the 11 IAD, the fighters then moved to Lida but were attacked by Junkers Ju 88s almost as soon as they landed, with the divisional loss of sixty nine I-16s. Even more tragic was the loss of many pilots including the divisional commander Colonel P. Ganichev.

One unit that escaped the first Luftwaffe attacks was the 43rd IAD commanded by a Spanish Civil War veteran Major General

**Sergeants Slesarchuk, Gozin and Perevera of the Moscow Air Defence District pose in front of an I-16 equipped with missile rails. Note the red star on the spinner.**

Starting the engine of an I-16 *tip* 17 with the help of a GAZ-AA or GAZ-MM 1.5-ton truck equipped with a Hucks starter.

Red Banner Baltic Fleet/13th OAE (Independent Air Squadron) pilots pose with an I-16 wearing squadron markings. Note the unusually small star on the tail.

Above: Lt. Krichevskiy (254th IAP, Leningrad Front) in his I-16 *tip* 24 '27 White/1 White' at Boodogoschch airfield; note the five 'kill' markings on the fuselage spine.

Red Banner Baltic Fleet/13th OAE crews rest after a practice alert in the summer of 1940. The real war is less than a year away.

Above: 16 White, the I-16 flown by ace Lt. (sg) Anatoliy G. Lomakin, on display at the Museum of the Defence of Leningrad in 1945., with an IL-2 in the background. Lomakin earned the Hero of the Soviet Union title on January 22, 1944 while serving as squadron vice-commander with the 21st IAP. He was killed in action three days later after scoring his 24th victory.

Red Banner Baltic Fleet Air Arm I-16s are prepared for a sortie in the autumn of 1943; the aircraft have warm engine covers to keep the engines from cooling while standing on ready alert.

Zakharov. It had four regiments: the 161st, 162nd and 163rd IAPs equipped exclusively with I-16s and the 160th IAP with I-153 biplanes. In total there were 175 I-16s and 60 I-153s. On 22nd June in defence of Minsk the divisional commander leading from the front personally shot down two Ju 88s. On the 24th June 163rd IAP destroyed 21 enemy aeroplanes. In a citation issued by the Commander-in-Chief of the Western Military District the 43rd IAD was praised for having flown 4,638 missions with a total duration of 5,956 hours in which 167 enemy aircraft were shot down for the loss of 26 in air battles and 63 on the ground.

The first VVS regiment to be awarded the honorary 'Guards' title was the 29th IAP (Red Banner). Operating in the Minsk area and flying the I-16 *tip* 24, it distinguished itself in many ground attack missions, as well as shooting down 67 enemy aeroplanes over a four-month period.

Although the I-16 was obsolescent and 100 km/h (62 mph) slower than the Messerschmitt Bf 109B, it was still a formidable opponent in the hands of a skilful pilot and could out-manoeuvre it in the horizontal plane. In fact, the variants with more powerful M-62 and M-63 engines (*tip* 18 and higher) could even match the Bf 109E in the vertical plane. Unfortunately the tactics used by Soviet pilots were ineffective as they usually flew in swarms of twelve aircraft in close rows. *Luftwaffe* pilots dived to the attack, flying straight through the formation with guns blazing, and then zoomed off to mount another attack from above, thus avoiding close combat.

Bombers did not provide easy targets for I-16 pilots. Junkers Ju 88s were faster than the I-16 and although the Heinkel He 111 was slower, its armour and self-sealing fuel tanks made it difficult to shoot down with the four 7.62 mm ShKAS machine-guns with which most I-16s were equipped.

The losses of the invaders mounted as they advanced swiftly into the USSR and by 19th July the *Luftwaffe* alone had lost 1,384 aircraft. Great as this figure appears, it dwindles into insignificance against Soviet losses which were increased by the necessity to use types such as the I-16 in ground attack roles where their lack of sufficient armour, coupled with the effective anti-aircraft defences of German infantry and panzer divisions, extracted a heavy toll. By July 1941 the *Luftwaffe* were in a position to bomb Moscow, but not before the VI Fighter Corps of the PVO (**Protivovozdooshnaya oborona**, Air Defence Force) entrusted with the defence of Moscow had been reinforced by 123 fighters increasing its total to 708, of which 233 were I-16s. This number continued to grow until a maximum of 783 fighters was achieved. The I-16 was operational with the following units on the 31st July 1941: the 16th IAP – a mixed regiment with MiG-3s at Lyubertsy and Bykovo; the 34th IAP – another mixed regiment at Klin; the 176th IAP at Stepykhino – an understrength unit totalling 20 fighters, of which five were I-153 biplanes and the rest I-16s; the 177th IAP at Doobrovitsy; the 233rd IAP at Tushino had a mix of MiG-3s, LaGG-3s and 18 I-16s; finally, at Ramenskoye there was a small mixed detachment including 4 I-16s.

On the night of 22nd July the *Luftwaffe* mounted its first major raid on Moscow with 250 bombers. PVO fighters attacked and dispersed them before they could reach the capital, shooting down twelve, a further ten falling to anti-aircraft guns. These night raids continued, with a further eighteen up to 15th August by which time the Soviets claimed to have destroyed about 200 German aircraft. It was not until the beginning of September that these heavy raids were reduced to desultory attacks by small numbers of bombers. By the beginning of October the number of I-16s defending Moscow had been reduced from 233 to 117 and had plunged to 90 by 1st December. In addition to losses due to enemy action many I-16s, as they were replaced by more modern fighters, were handed over to regiments serving with the frontal armies so that by autumn 1942 a mere 13 remained with VI Air Defence Corps, and even these had disappeared by the spring of 1943.

**At least two UTI-4 coded DM+HC (illustrated) and DM+HD were evaluated by the *Luftwaffe*'s test centre (*Erprobungsstelle* Rechlin).**

An I-16 *tip* 17, one of the few surviving genuine I-16s, in the Navy Museum in St. Petersburg.

Technicians make repairs to the damaged wing root fairing of an I-16 in field conditions.

Polikarpov's little monoplane fighters were in action on all fronts from Murmansk in the north to the Black Sea in the south and it was at these extreme edges of the USSR that the Naval Air Arm made its contribution to victory.

For the defence of Leningrad the VII Fighter Corps of the PVO had been formed with 232 fighters, of which 149 (ie, 64%) were I-16s. By the end of 1941 the city was surrounded on land by German and Finnish armies and the PVO units were now supported by the remaining aircraft of the Black Sea Fleet and the Military District. One of their key tasks was to keep open the aerial supply line by which transport aircraft flew in supplies to beat the blockade of the besieged city. Involved in this effort was the 286 IAP which was only formed in June 1941 and whose I-16s were flown by young sergeants with only three months' flying experience. Although pitted against Messerschmitt Bf 109s, they fought bravely and most of the transports got through. In the fourteen months of defending this airlift the regiment led by Major P. Baranov shot down 44 enemy aircraft.

An outstanding naval regiment was the 13th IAP of the Baltic Fleet based on the Hanko peninsula in the Gulf of Finland to defend the ships and garrison based there. Rendered vulnerable by being within range of Finnish artillery, its aircraft were housed in underground hangars. One distinguished pilot was Aleksey Antonenko who shot down eleven aircraft between his arrival on the 25th June 1941 and his death from a mortar bomb whilst landing on 25th July. By the end of the year the position had become untenable and the regiment moved to a base at Karbona, an important entrepot on the route over the frozen Lake Ladoga to blockaded Leningrad. The regiment's new role was to defend this route from air attack. So important was it to the starving people of Leningrad that it became known as the 'Road of Life'.

By the middle of March 1942 the regiment had been awarded the coveted *Gvardeyskiy* (Guards, used attributively) title, becoming the 4th GvIAP; regiments were always renumbered when receiving this honour. Between 12th March and 13th April it had destroyed 54 enemy aircraft for the loss of only two I-16s. One flight commander flying this type of aircraft, Captain Victor Golubev, a Hero of the Soviet Union, personally accounted for 27 'kills' by the end of 1943, including two Focke-Wulf Fw 190s; his final score after transitioning to the Lavochkin La-5 was 39. Many attacks usually by about 50 enemy aircraft were fought off and two more flight commanders became 'Heroes of the Soviet Union'. The regiment was one of the last operational units to retain the I-16, keeping it until the end of 1943.

Another famous naval regiment was the 72nd IAP in which Senior Lt Boris Safonov had claimed the first enemy aircraft to be shot down in the Northern Sector, around Murmansk – an He 111. He went on to become the most successful fighter pilot in this sector destroying 17 enemy machines in 109 sorties before his much worn I-16 (construction number 2821309) was exchanged for a Hawker Hurricane. Promoted to Major, he commanded the 72 IAP, now honoured as the 2 GvIAP, and was ultimately credited with 25 enemy aircraft and 14 shared kills before being killed in action while defending convoy PQ 14. He was the first Soviet pilot to become a 'Hero of the Soviet Union' twice over.

Defending Odessa, the 69th IAP was commanded by Major Leonid Shestakov. Its claim to fame was the pioneering use of RS-82 rockets on its I-16s. These weapons were used successfully against ground targets as well as aircraft. The main foe in this sector was the Romanian Air Force which was using Polish-built PZL-24 fighters capable of out-turning the I-16s. However, combat records of the 69th IAP show the destruction of 94 aeroplanes and 3 gliders before its final evacuation from the city. Twelve pilots were simultaneously recommended to be recognised as 'Heroes of the Soviet Union', five posthumously. The regimental commander who had shot down three aircraft and shared in the destruction of eight more was also decorated.

As the war progressed the number of I-16s in use rapidly diminished as heavy losses were not replaced by new aircraft. Production of fighter variants had stopped in 1941 in which year only 99 were built whilst factories changed over to more modern designs. For example, the AVMF had 91 on 1st May 1942 and by the middle of the year this number had halved to 46 and continued to decrease until, by the beginning of 1944, there was only one left. A similar pattern occurred in the VVS whose frontal regiments possessed 240 I-16s at the end of 1941 but only 42 in operational use by 1st July 1943, a number representing 1% of the fighter force. It seems to have been policy to withdraw the I-16 from front-line units and Moscow PVO as quickly as possible and pass serviceable ones over to other PVO units where its numbers actually increased from 333 at the beginning of 1942 to 348 six months later. But by the end of 1943 this number had fallen to 42 and in 1944 the I-16 was withdrawn from operational use in the west by all three air arms.

Probably the last operational I-16 unit was the 888th IAP based at Petropavlovsk-Kamchatskiy where, until August 1945, it fought off Japanese fighters which were attacking stray American bombers. It was then re-equipped with Bell P-63 Kingcobras and no I-16s were used in the attack on Japanese-occupied Manchuria on 9th August 1945.

*Zveno*-SPB composite aircraft were operated in the south of the country by the Black Sea Fleet and used to attack especially important and heavily guarded targets. This was a novel scheme and one well worth a special mention. The *Zveno* composite was developed by Vladimir Vakhmistrov before the war and the final configuration consisted of a Tupolev TB-3 four-engined bomber with a modified I-16 *tip* 5 (unofficially called I-16SPB) under each wing. These fighter bombers each carried two underwing 250 kg (550 lb) bombs with which they could not take off unaided. A mother-ship was used to carry them as close to the target area as was possible without attracting enemy fighters. It then released the I-16s which, after destroying the target, would have sufficient fuel to fly back to base. At least that was the theory (and one which was rejected by the VVS). However, the Navy had one regiment of Zveno-SPBs, the 32nd BAP (*bombardirovochnyy aviatsionnyy polk*, Bomber aviation regiment) of the Black Sea Fleet, based at Yevpatoria in the Crimea. On 26th July 1941 (some sources give 1st August) two *Zveno*-SPB composite aircraft took off to attack oil depots in Constantsa, Romania. Released from the TB-3 at 4,000m (13,000 ft) and 35 km (21 miles) from the target, they achieved a surprise attack, confounding the enemy who were not expecting to see Soviet fighters 350 km (220 miles) from the border. Four Messerschmitt fighters flew by unalerted and there was no AA gunfire. Diving from 2,000 m (6,500 ft), the bombs were released at 800 m (2,600 ft) and struck their target. Three I-16 returned safely to refuel at Odessa before returning home the fourth ran out of fuel just short of Odessa and made a forced landing damaging the aircraft and injuring the pilot. This was an historic first military use of parasite aircraft.

To accomplish their next mission it was necessary for the I-16s to carry under-fuselage 95 litre (20 gal.) fuel tanks. Their new target at Chernavoda was the only bridge over the Danube in Romania which formed a crucial link in the enemy supply route for their invading armies. So important was it that the AA gunners were ordered to fire at any aircraft within a 10 km (6 mile) radius! To wear down the defences it was planned for DB-3 bombers to bombard the bridge throughout the night before the main attack was to take place. Once again two *Zveno*-SPB composites took off, this time at 3.10am on 10th August. Once released, the I-16 pressed on to the target over which the bombs were released at a height of 600 m (2,000 ft), scoring three direct hits, but the bridge, although damaged, remained intact. A second attack took place on 13th August, scoring five direct hits. One truss of the bridge was completely destroyed together with 605m (2130 ft) of the oil pipeline and all without any loss to the Soviet side.

A second, less successful raid on Constantsa was undertaken on the 17th August by two composites. This time the target was the floating dock in which destroyers were being repaired. No direct hits were obtained but 'the dock was filled with water' and two of the I-16s were lost.

The last distant raid by the *Zveno*-SPB composites was on 20th August 1941 when two attacked a bridge over the Dnieper near Zaporozh'ye. On this mission they were escorted to the target by 24 I-16s. Although five bombs hit and destroyed the upper span carrying the railway the bombs were not large enough to penetrate as far as the lower road span which survived undamaged. After this raid the composites were used to get the I-16SPB airborne for local attacks on the advancing German army and pontoon bridges until 22nd October 1941 when the remnants of the regiment were withdrawn to the Caucasus.

**Survivors**
Special mention must be made of the six flying I-16s – the only flying examples of the type in the world – professionally restored for the Alpine Fighter Collection in New Zealand by SibNIA in 1995-98. The applicability of the term 'restored' is questionable, since, though the fighters **do** make use of original components recovered in north-western Russia, they are effectively new-build aircraft – in other words, flying replicas. (A comment about the axe which was used to behead Mary Queen of Scots, and is now in a museum, comes to mind: 'It may have had three new handles and two new heads in the meantime, but it is still the same axe. Or is it?')

Originally pertaining to various versions of the I-16 (as could be ascertained from manufacturer plates on the wreckage), all six aircraft were completed to *tip* 24 standard. After being test-flown in Novosibirsk in 1995-98 they were shipped to Wanaka, New Zealand, reassembled and reflown, gaining civil registrations and certificates of airworthiness in the experimental category.

The cost of the deal was not disclosed, but the Russian daily *Kommersant* quoted a price of US$300,000 for an I-16 on the Western warbird market.

The fighters are powered by ASh-62IR engines driving AV-1M all-metal two-blade propellers. All have been fitted with IImorrow Apollo SL40 radios and Artex ELT 200 GPS receivers. Their top speed was limited to 430 km/h (267 mph), but this was expected to be increased to 460 km/h (285 mph).

The registrations were worn visibly at first but promptly vanished so as not to spoil the authenticity. Yet this was ruined again when the owner, wishing to give the aircraft a more 'warbirdlike' look, painted the slogan *Za Baletkora* on both sides of '4 Red' without taking the trouble to look at real Soviet 'graffiti' of the period. There is no such Russian word as *baletkor*; this can be translated as 'ballet correspondent', which of course does not make sense.

It is reportedly the intention of the AFC to sell three of the four I-16s that they currently possess.

I-16s on display are, with three exceptions, replicas and all known ones are listed below:

| Version | Markings/serial (side number) | Location | Notes |
|---|---|---|---|
| I-16 *tip* 10 | Soviet | Valeriy P. Chkalov Museum, Chkalovsk, Russia | Genuine |
| I-16 *tip* 24 | Soviet | Naval Museum, Leningrad (now St Petersburg, Russia) | Genuine |
| I-16 *tip* 6 | Soviet | Soviet (now Russian) Air Force Museum, Monino, Russia | Replica |
| I-16 *tip* 10 | Soviet (91 White) | Great Patriotic War Museum, Moscow, Russia | Replica |
| I-16 | Soviet | Northern Fleet Museum, Severomorsk, Russia | Replica with some original salvaged parts |
| UTI-4 | Finnish (UT-1) | Finnish Aviation Museum, Helsinki-Vantaa Airport, Finland | Genuine |
| I-16 | Spanish (CM-260/C.8-25) | Air Museum, Madrid-Cuatro Vientos International Airport, Spain | Replica – one side in Republican markings, the other in Nationalist markings |
| I-16 *tip* 10 | Chinese (5806 White) | People's Liberation Army Air Force Museum, Datangshan, China | Replica |

**The six flying I-16s restored for the Alpine Fighter Collection during 1995-1998 are:**

| Side number/ Registration | Construction number* | Location | Notes |
|---|---|---|---|
| 9 Red (ZK-JIN) | 2421319 | Alpine Fighter Collection, Lake Wanaka, NZ | Original aircraft built by Plant No. 21 late 1939 or early 1940, possibly *tip* 18 partly upgraded to *tip* 24 standard. Believed operated by the 155th IAP, North Fleet Air Arm; crashed 2 km NW of Lake Kokkoyarvi (38 km SW of Kostomooksha, Karelia) in 1941 or 1942. First post-reconstruction flight 1995. Green with light blue undersurfaces, white fin cap |
| 28 White (ZK-JIR) | 2421645 | Lone Star Flight Museum, Galveston, Texas, USA (ex-Alpine Fighter Collection) | Original aircraft built by Plant No. 21 in 1939, believed operated by the 155th IAP; crashed at Nigizero village near Kondopoga, Karelia, in 1941 or 1942. Wreckage discovered in 1991; first post-reconstruction flight 1996. Black/green camouflage with light grey undersurfaces; marked 2421028 on tail in error |
| 34 Red (ZK-JIO) | 2421028 | Alpine Fighter Collection | Original aircraft built by Plant No. 21 in 1940 (?), version unknown. Believed operated by the 197th IAP, crashed near Orzega, Karelia, in 1941. Wreckage discovered in 1988; first post-reconstruction flight 1996. Silver overall; marked 2421234 on tail in error |
| 45 White (ZK-JIP) | 2421014 | Lone Star Flight Museum (ex-Alpine Fighter Collection) | Original aircraft built by Plant No. 21 in 1939 (?), believed operated by Baltic Fleet Air Arm/Leningrad Front, crashed 500 m from the settlement of Osinovets (Leningrad Region). Wreckage discovered in 1991; first post-reconstruction flight 1997. Two-tone green camouflage with light grey undersurfaces |
| 4 Red (ZK-JIQ) | 2421234 | Alpine Fighter Collection | Original aircraft built by Plant No. 21 as *tip* 29, crashed north-west of Lake Yaglyarvi, Karelia. Wreckage discovered in 1991; first post-reconstruction flight 1997. Green with black cowling and light grey undersurfaces; marked 2421014 on tail in error |
| 239 White (ZK-JJC) | 2421039 | Alpine Fighter Collection | Original aircraft built by Plant No. 21 in 1937 (*tip* 5), upgraded to *tip* 24 standard (had M-62 engine c/n 623358). Believed operated by the 155th IAP, North Fleet Air Arm; crashed near Lake Kokkoyarvi between 1941 and 1943. Wreckage discovered in 1992; first post-reconstruction flight 1998. Black/green camouflage with light blue undersurfaces |

\* The construction numbers reflecting the version (*tip* 24) are not real in most cases because the aircraft are composites of various *tips*.

Chapter 7

# The 'Super-*Ishachok*'

## And Other Successors

The **I-180** (*'samolyot* **Ye**', *tip* **25**) was designed to take into account the lessons of the Spanish Civil war which was still raging in March 1938 when the preliminary work on this design was completed. It was hoped to produce a fighter as close as possible to the design of the I-16 (hence it was sometimes referred to as the 'Super-*Ishachok*') but the required top speed of 600 km/h (373 mph) was not attainable with an existing Soviet radial engine. At first it had been hoped to use the 930 hp (693 kw) M-87A designed by A. S. Nazarov at the OKB of *zavod* 29 at Zaporozh'ye in the Ukraine and preliminary work started on aircraft type Ye but it soon became apparent that this would not give a fast enough top speed. An alternative engine had to be found and the most suitable available at that time was the 960 hp (716 kW) M-88 double-row radial with fuel injection estimated to give a maximum speed of 557 km/h (346 mph); it was expected to be developed to give 1,100 hp (820 kW). However, it was a much heavier and bulkier engine than the M-63 used in the last model of the I-16 and a considerable amount of redesigning was necessary before it could be installed to give an optimum position for the centre of gravity.

A fuselage over half a metre longer was built using a similar type of wooden monocoque construction with a circular cross section. A pneumatically retractable landing gear was designed and the open cockpit was raised 155 mm (6 in.) to improve the pilot's view. The wings had a higher aspect ratio than the I-16 and were given a straight rather than a swept back leading edge to help mitigate against the heavier engine; a Clark-YH profile and the customary KhMA steel spars were used with duralumin leading edges to which was riveted the adhesive tape securing the fabric covering the rest of the wing. A beam was secured under each wing to allow the carriage of two drop tanks or four bombs of maximum total weight of 200 kg (440 lb). Two 7.62 mm ShKAS machine guns were located in the nose and two more in the wings having a total of 2,320 rounds.

The I-180-1 (production code Ye-1), the first prototype, was assembled for its maiden flight on 15th December 1938 but lacked armament. It had the prototype M-88 engine which was assembled using M-87A components, but instead of the intended variable-pitch propeller one of fixed pitch had to be used. Furthermore, the adjustable gills for controlling the engine's cooling system were not fitted. Only a few ground runs had been made with the engine and on 12th December, whilst the prototype was undergoing its first high speed taxiing trials, an engine control rod broke. Although this part was quickly replaced, the ground testing programme for the Ye-1 was not completed before the first flight. Therefore it was decided not to retract the undercarriage which was locked in the down position

After inspecting the aircraft the test pilot Valeriy Chkalov, took off. Instead of completing a single circuit he did several until, tragically, whilst performing a descending turn on finals, an engine seizure caused him to crash into storage facilities at the edge of the airfield; the pilot was thrown clear of the aircraft, sustaining fatal injuries. Chkalov had earned acclaim for his long-range flights, becoming a national hero, and was a particular favourite of Stalin. Sabotage was alleged and several prominent people were arrested including Polikarpov's deputy Dmitriy L. Tomashevich who was the chief designer of the aircraft. By

The I-180-2 (second prototype I-180); note forward gills regulating the flow of cooling air over the engine. The aircraft can best be described as an extremely improved I-16. Unfortunately no photographs have survived of the first prototype.

These views show well the I-180-2's long-chord cowling with exhaust stubs all around.

The third prototype, I-180-3, as originally flown with an open cockpit. Here, the aircraft is shown on skis. The restyled engine cowling is well visible.

Above: This rare view illustrates the I-180's wing planform with unswept leading edge and sharply swept-forward trailing edge.

The I-180-3 trestled for landing gear retraction tests; the skis are just visible under the wing centre section. The ink stamp in the upper left corner reads *Sekretno* (Classified).

Above: The cockpit of the I-180-3.

The I-180-3's tail unit.

Above and below: The I-180-3 after installation of an aft-sliding cockpit canopy. The aircraft appears to have been given a new coat of paint, too.

chance Polikarpov had not given his written permission for the flight and so was not arrested; Tomashevich was not so fortunate and was sent to the TsKB *sharahga* (prison OKB) in *zavod* 39. It seemed likely that the primary cause of the engine failure was overcooling during the landing approach. On the fateful day the air temperature at ground level was -25°C (-13°F) and there were no gills to close to keep the engine warm (these were envisaged by the project but not fitted in time for the first flight).

After it had been established that no design fault had caused the crash, work started on building the second prototype, I-180-2 (or Ye-2). By then the OKB had moved to the larger *Zavod* 1 *imeni Aviakhima*. A more reliable but less powerful motor was used, a production 930 hp (693 kW) M-87A with a 2.9 m (9.5 ft) VISh-23 variable-pitch propeller. Wingspan was lengthened to 10.1 m (33.1 ft) with a corresponding increase in wing area. This time the intended armament of four ShKAS machine-guns was installed. Stepan P. Sooproon made a successful first flight on either the 19 or 27th April 1939, the doubt arises from conflicting sources, some of whom suggest that only taxiing trials took place on the first mentioned date; understandably the preparations for this event were very thorough. After Sooproon had flown the I-180-2 in the May Day flypast over Red Square it was discovered on landing that the skin on the wings had started to buckle. Flight tests were then stopped until this was remedied. With a take-off weight of 2,370 kg (5,224 lb) the maximum speed was 408 km/h (253 mph) at sea level and 540 km/h (335 mph) at 5,850 m (19,200 ft); the time taken to climb to 5,000 m (16,400 ft) was 6.25 minutes and it had a service ceiling of 10,250 m (33,600 ft). These performance figures were well below design estimates for the I-180 because of the use of a lower powered engine. More rigid outer wing panels with smooth metal skins were fitted and the engine, which had only logged 10 hours, was exchanged for the slightly more powerful 950 hp (708 kW) M-87B featuring cooling gills at the front. Test pilots Pyotr M. Stefanovskiy, S. P. Sooproon and Tomas P. Suzi flew the aircraft when flight tests resumed on 8th August.

Another successful public appearance for the I-180-2 took place at Tushino during the flypast for Air Force Day on 18th August 1939. But tragedy struck again during its 53rd flight on 5th September when the service ceiling with the new engine was being determined. At 9,000 m (29,500 ft) the oil cooler collapsed and T. Suzi, burnt and blinded by oil, lost control and baled out but was too seriously injured to deploy his parachute and he fell to his death. The oil cooler that collapsed was of a new circular design fashionable in the West. It was situated immediately behind the spinner with the oil flowing through concentric rings cooled by the incoming air.

However, some of the engineers – and Polikarpov himself – had different views. They claimed Suzi had lost consciousness at high altitude due a malfunction in the oxygen equipment, his head hanging over the side of the cockpit. (This was based on the fact that there had been trouble with the oxygen equipment on earlier flights.) A while later the oil cooler indeed failed, as the engine was running at full power. The hot oil was splashed in the pilot's face; regaining consciousness from the pain, he tried to regain control but could see nothing and the aircraft flipped into a spin. Suzi may have lost consciousness again after baling out, hence his failure to open his parachute.

The loss of two prototypes and the deaths of two famous test pilots dealt a crippling blow to the prestige of the Polikarpov Design Bureau and it is believed that it was at this time that the chief designer fell out of favour with Stalin. However work on the I-180 was allowed to continue because neither crash was attributed to bad airframe design.

The I-180-3 (production code Ye-3), the third prototype, was assembled with the 1,000hp (746 kW) M-88R engine and with two of the 7.62 mm machine-guns replaced by two 12.7 mm UBS type designed by M. Berezin which were provided with 470 rounds each. All four guns were now placed in the fuselage nose. To accommodate the new VISh-23E variable-pitch propeller of 3.0m (9.8 ft) diameter the undercarriage was moved forward and its legs lengthened. A new type of oil cooler of a honeycomb construction was re-located to a duct under the engine.

The first flight took place on 10th February 1940 with Yevgeniy Oolyakhin at the controls and tests continued until 18th May during which time the cockpit was enclosed and given a rearward sliding canopy; a larger tail plane was also fitted. There had been a narrow escape from damaging the aircraft when on 20th February the starboard undercarriage leg failed to lock down on landing. Fortunately whilst attempting to land on only the port leg the malfunctioning leg locked on touchdown, enabling, at the last moment, a safe landing. Compared with the second prototype, take-off weight had increased to 2,424 kg (5,343 lb) but, in spite of this, maximum speed had increased to 455 km/h (282 mph) at sea level

**Close-up of the third prototype's new canopy.**

One of the few surviving photos of an intact production I-180S (*izdeliye* 25) built in Gor'kiy. Unfortunately one of the propeller blades has 'disappeared' due to the poor quality of the photo.

and 575 km/h (357 mph) at 6,900 m (22,600 ft); the I-180-3 also climbed to 5,000 m (16,400 ft) in only 5.8 minutes and the service ceiling had increased to 11,050 m (36,250 ft).

On completing its factory trials and subsequent modifications the third prototype went in June 1940 to the NII VVS for State Acceptance Tests which were conducted by test pilot Afanasiy Proshakov. It was there that the enlarged tail plane showed signs of flutter and was replaced by the previous one. On the 5th July the controls failed during aerobatics and Proshakov could not recover the aircraft from an inverted position; fortunately he managed to parachute to safety.

In spite of the appaling record of two prototypes and two test pilots lost (the third prototype at this time had yet to crash), the aircraft was scheduled for series production at *zavod* 21 in Gor'kiy. Series aircraft had the constructor's designation 'type 25' and were to be called **I-180S** (*sereeynyy*, series) in VVS service. The factory, however, would have preferred to give priority to the I-21 fighter developed at their own design department under the leadership of Mikhail M. Pashinin, but under official pressure ten examples of the I-180S were belatedly and grudgingly assembled; six were sent to the NII VVS and of the other four, three were seen over Red Square in the 1940 May Day parade.

On the 26th May the second I-180S (construction number 25212) crash-landed at Khodynka after a checkout flight. The starboard main gear unit's torque link failed on touchdown and the wheel turned 90° (another possibility is that the pilot had to brake hard to avoid another aircraft taxiing out in front and the fighter swung). Anyway, the fighter dug in its wingtip and somersaulted; the pilot, S. P. Sooproon, was unhurt but the aircraft was a write-off.

Modifications were planned at a meeting at the factory when Polikarpov agreed that the next production batch should have the following modifications: enclosed cockpits, the new M-88A engines, RSI-4 radios complete with aerials, single leg undercarriages and the provision for unguided missiles and 200 litre (44 gals) drop tanks. Before further aircraft could be built the NKAP in October 1940 instructed the factory to increase output of the I-16 and prepare for the production of another type, the LaGG-3, and series production of the I-180 was abandoned.

The **I-180Sh** (*shassee*, undercarriage) or **I-184** was the designation given to an aircraft which was experimentally given a single cantilever strut for each undercarriage leg instead of the customary three. It was planned to install this type in all series production at *zavod* 21 from the 31st aircraft.

Production totalled thirteen; one from the experimental *zavod* 156, two from *zavod* 1 and ten from *zavod* 21. Some historians suggest that not all the last ten aircraft were completed to flying condition and were scrapped in the factory.

In July 1940 Polikarpov, and what was left of his OKB, were transferred to a new experimental factory designated *zavod* 51; it was originally intended to be *zavod* 100 but this number had already been given to another experimental plant in Leningrad. This small establishment, close to *zavod* 1, in the Khodinka suburb of Moscow, was a rebuilt workshop previously used by TsAGI. Humble though his new premises were, at least Polikarpov had the satisfaction of being the master of his own ship because he was appointed both Factory Director and Chief Designer. Here he continued his design work on the TIS twin-engined and I-185 and ITP single-engined fighters and the ODB bomber.

The **I-185** (*izdeliye* 62) was now to be the replacement for the I-180 and hopefully

**Data for the I-180**

|  | I-180-2 | I-180-3 | I-180S |
| --- | --- | --- | --- |
| Span | 10.09 m | 10.09 m | 10.09 m |
|  | (33.1 ft) | (33.1 ft) | (33.1 ft) |
| Length | 6.79 m | 6.88 m | 6.88 m |
|  | (22.3 ft) | (22.6 ft) | (22.6 ft) |
| Wing area | 16.11 m$^2$ | 16.11 m$^2$ | 16.11 m$^2$ |
|  | (173 ft$^2$) | (173 ft$^2$) | (173 ft$^2$) |
| Empty weight | 1,847 kg | 2,020 kg | 2,046 kg |
|  | (4,072 lb) | (4,453 lb) | (4,511 lb) |
| Take-off weight | 2,370 kg | 2,424 kg | 2,456 kg |
|  | (5,224 lb) | (5,343 lb) | (5,414 lb) |
| Fuel | 200 kg | 200 kg | 200 kg |
|  | (440 lb) | (440 lb) | (440 lb) |
| Top speed at sea level | 408 km/h | 455 km/h | 470 km/h |
|  | (253 mph) | (282 mph) | (292 mph) |
| Top speed at height | 540 km/h | 575 km/h | 585 km/h |
|  | (335 mph) | (357 mph) | (364 mph) |
| Climb to 5,000 m | 6.25 mins | 5.8 mins | 5.0 mins |
| Service ceiling | 10,250 m | 11,050 m | n.a |
|  | (33,630 ft) | (36,250 ft) |  |
| Range | 800 km | 900 km | n.a |
|  | (500 miles) | (560 miles) |  |
| Time to turn 360° | 21 secs | 19.5 secs | n.a |
| Take off run | n.a | 240 m | n.a |
|  |  | (787 ft) |  |
| Landing run | n.a | 200 m | n.a |
|  |  | (656 ft) |  |
| Landing speed | n.a | 130 km/h | n.a |
|  |  | (81 mph) |  |

Above and below: This I-180S (c/n 25212) flipped over at Moscow-Khodynka airfield during manufacturer's flight tests when an undercarriage leg failed. The pilot walked away but the aircraft broke its back aft of the wings and was a write-off.

Секретно.

Above and below: Ducted spinners of 380mm (14.96 in.) and 500 mm (19.68 in.) diameter were tried for the I-180 in the wind tunnel. Note the exhaust stacks looking as if an inline or V-12 engine was installed.

A mockup of the M-90-powered I-180 tested in a TsAGI wind tunnel. Note the airflow visualization threads on the wings and the ducted spinner.

successor to the I-16. After Polikarpov had been ordered to hand over further design and development work on the *Samolyot* Kh to the Mikoyan design team he turned his attention once again to a radial engine for a new fighter he was designing at experimental *zavod* 51. As was his custom, he selected the latest but untried engine to power his brainchild. In this instance he selected the 18-cylinder Nazarov M-90 still under development which had an optimistically projected take-off rating of 2,000hp (1,492 kW); an optimism which was soon shown to be misplaced. It is impossible not to admire his bravery, some might even say foolhardiness, in deciding yet again on a brand-new and not fully proved engine. He had, however, placed himself in a cleft stick; there was little point in designing a fighter incapable of matching the best international competition, the Bf 109 and the Spitfire. Therefore in order to accomplish this aim he needed a more powerful engine than any that had reached the stage of being considered reliable. To maximise performance and improve engine cooling Polikarpov had selected a new close-fitting cowling with a ducted spinner and fan, the air after cooling the cylinders was expelled through gills giving extra thrust.

Structurally the I-185 was similar to the I-180, with a monocoque *shpon* fuselage and integral tailfin. A broad enclosed cockpit had a shallow windscreen with the canopy sliding backwards. To reduce drag a small wing with an area of 15.53 sq. m was used with very thin aerofoil sections; 13% at the root and 8% at the tips. This was nearly as thin as the Spitfire's wing (at that time the thinnest on contemporary fighters), and to withstand the higher wing loading a new stronger all-metal two-spar wing with NACA-230 profile was designed with a high aspect ratio of 6.18 and covered with duralumin stressed skin. Four-section split fabric-covered ailerons and automatic slats were pneumatically operated and these devices counteracted the high wing loading to allow a reasonable landing speed of 132 km/h (82 mph), which was 10 km/h slower than the Lavochkin La-5FN would have with a much lower wing loading. Elevators and the cantilever tailplane were made of duralumin with the control surfaces fabric covered but the tailfin was wooden and an integral part of the fuselage. One interesting feature was an oil cooler duct centrally placed under the wing centre section situated almost as far back as the cabin. The single-leg main undercarriage had air and hydraulic damping and a 2.7 m (8.9 ft) track with 700 x 220 mm wheels retracting inwards to give the appearance of a small blister close to the wing root. A retractable castoring tailwheel was installed which could be locked for take-off.

The gun armament was to comprise two 7.62 mm ShKAS and two 12.7 mm UBS machine guns, and under overload conditions the fighter could carry a 500 kg (1,100 lb) bomb. Estimated top speed was 715 km/h (444 mph) at 7,300 m (24,000 ft) and the service ceiling 10,250 m (33,600ft).

In May 1940 the aircraft was ready but the engine, during both bench tests and taxiing trials, did not give sufficient power for take-off. In desperation another new experimental engine, the 1,200hp (895 kW) Shvetsov M-81, was tried. This low-power motor allowed only one short flight on 11th January 1941 to be made before a decision was taken to cut their losses and wait for an engine with sufficient power. In May 1941 the authorities lost patience and further development and series production of the M-81 was cancelled. A second prototype had been completed at the end of 1940 and tried with the new 14 cylinder 1,700 hp (1,268 kW) Shvetsov M-82A. One advantage of this engine was its small 126 cm (50 in.) diameter which appreciably reduced the aircraft's drag. It was also decided to change the armament from four machineguns to three 20 mm ShVAK cannons all mounted in the nose with a total of 500 rounds. Flight tests of this aeroplane started in May 1941.

The third prototype was given the 18 cylinder 2,000 hp (1,492 kW) Shvetsov M-71 motor. Eight rods forming a frame were used for mounting the engine, which was angled 25 mm (one inch) down relative to the aircraft's longitudinal axis. Testing of the M-71 powered

Another full-scale mockup of the M-90-powered I-180 in a different TsAGI wind tunnel. Note the clipped wings (otherwise the aircraft would not fit in).

An artist's impression of the DIT-185, a projected trainer version of the M-90-powered I-180.

**Above and below:** The M-71-powered I-185 as flown in 1941. The aircraft bears a striking resemblance to the Lavockhkin La-5 which appeared in 1943; performance was very similar, too.

prototype was interrupted by the German invasion and the subsequent evacuation of *zavod* 51 and the OKB to Novosibirsk. These tests proved to be successful enough for the first prototype to be re-engined with the M-71.

Test pilot P. Loginov from the factory, as well as A. Nikashin and L. Koovshinov of the NII VVS, conducted performance tests on the I-185 M-71 and armament trials on the I-185 M-82A. One interesting result was that Polikarpov was instructed to pass on to the OKBs of Lavochkin, Mikoyan and Yakovlev the drawings for the M-82A engine installation and the cannon mountings. An associated consequence was that development of the La-5 and the experimental Yak-7/M-82A, both of which had the same M-82A engine, was accelerated.

By common consent the M-71 variant was a better proposition than the prototype with the M-82A engine and the test report suggested its superiority to all current production aircraft. It had been tested against the Yak-7B, LaGG-3, Bf 109F, He 100, Supermarine Spitfire and Bell P-39 Airacobra. At 3,485 kg (7,683 lb) it had a top speed at sea level of 556 km/h (345 mph) and this rose to 630 km/h (391 mph) at 6,170 m (20,250 ft). The Bf 109F was 47 km/h (29 mph) slower at sea level and 20 km/h (12 mph) slower at 6,000 m (19,700 ft).

96

Two rare views of the 1941-standard I-185.

The I-185 with an M-82A engine during manufacturer's flight tests.

The more elegant lines of the M-82A-powered version are evident in this view. Nevertheless, the aircraft had worse performance than the original M-71-powered version.

Above and below: Port and starboard views of the M-71-powered I-185 *etalon* (production standard-setter) for 1942.

Also, the time needed to reach 5,000 m (16,400) was 6.3 minutes, ie, 1.1 minutes greater. The I-185 M-71 was recommended for immediate production with the comment that its operation was within the capabilities of pilots of low proficiency.

All three prototypes were thoroughly tested under service conditions in November 1942 at the 728th IAP of the 3rd Air Army whose commander Captain Vasilyaka subsequently praised their superiority over current Soviet and foreign fighters, praise which encompassed not only speed, rate of climb and manoeuvrability, particularly in the vertical plane, but also their simpler construction, heavier armament and ability to survive battle damage. These tests were conducted, usually from Staritsa airfield on the Kalinin front, under very special conditions devised to guarantee as far as humanly possible the safety of the prototypes. The hand-picked pilots D. Koopin, N. Ignat'yev, A. Borovykh and A. Tomil'chenko and mechanics were introduced to the aircraft by Polikarpov himself. Sorties required the express permission of the 3rd Air Army staff and were strictly confined to be over Soviet-held territory. They took the form of a high-speed sweep down through previously detected enemy formations which were attacked with cannon fire during the pass, after which the I-185 immediately returned to base.

The only criticisms of the aircraft were the optical distortion through the windscreen, difficulty in operating the radiator blinds and the awkward position of the throttle lever.

In Spring 1942, long before these tests started, a decision was made to series produce the I-185 M-71. A production standard prototype (*etalon*) had been built and factory tested between June and October before proceeding to the NII VVS for State Trials on 18th November. To reduce drag a new engine cowling was fitted and this more than compensated for the 144 kg (317 lb) weight increase and the top speed under short boost rose to 600 km/h (372 mph) at sea level and 650 km/h (403 mph) at 6,100 m (20,000 ft). Range was 800 km (497 miles).

Again fulsome praise was lavished on it by the test pilot, P. Stefanovskiy and the NII VVS commander Major-General P. Losyukov who insisted that the fighter be introduced into the inventory of the VVS as 'it surpasses

**Top: The I-185 M-82 with the cowling doors open. Note that the outer wings have been removed.**

**Bottom: The I-185 *etalon* with the M-71 engine uncowled, showing the port synchronised ShVAK cannon.**

Photographs on the opposite page:
**The I-185's instrument panel.**

in maximum speed, climb rate and vertical manoeuvrability both the latest Soviet and foreign fighters in production'. Unfortunately, the engine did not live up to the same ideals and testing was delayed by frequent engine failures and a replacement engine failed after less than 24 hours of running. This problem culminated in the death of test pilot V. Stepanchonok on 27th January 1943 when he attempted a dead-stick landing and crashed into a hangar after yet another engine failure and planned production of the I-185 was cancelled in spite of several plants having spare capacity. The alternative powerplant, the M-82, was not considered as its production was earmarked for the new Lavochkin La-5 about to be built at *zavod* 21, Gor'kiy. On reflection it would appear that, at the eleventh hour, the authorities decided it was better to extend production of the La-5 which was a radial-engined version of the LaGG-3, a type that had been series produced since 1941 by three plants (in fact four plants had started but *zavod* 23 at Leningrad had been evacuated into Novosibirsk *zavod* 153). Another factor that could have influenced them was the La-5's use of less duralumin, a commodity in short supply at that time.

It is impossible not to pity Polikarpov who was yet again denied series production of one of his designs because of unreliable aeroengines. At the same time the decision taken not to build more I-185s would appear to have been correct, taken as it was, in 1943 when maximisation of the production of capable fighters was the overriding consideration. If a reliable engine had been available in 1941 or 1942 the argument for series production of the I-185s would have been overwhelming; unfortunately it was 1943 before that decision could be taken. Some historians believe that A. S. Yakovlev, then a Deputy Commissar and responsible for 'Experimental Aircraft Development', and himself a designer of rival fighters was able to influence the decision to further his own career. However, whilst it is just possible that this was his motive, it is unlikely that Stalin, who made the final fateful decision to cancel production, would have been influenced by such a transparent manoeuvre.

Polikarpov did not accept the decision without a fight and wrote to the Central Committee, pointing out that several aircraft plants were currently idle and able to change over very quickly to the I-185, but his protest fell on deaf ears.

The **I-186** is suggested by some historians to have been the proposed designation for the production standard I-185 M-71 (*etalon*).

The **I-187** was a projected improved version of the I-185 designed before development of the latter type was abandoned.

An artist's impression of the projected I-187; note the unusual design of the cooling gills.

An artist's impression of the projected I-188. This aircraft was to have an M-90 engine but a more streamlined cowling than the I-180.

An artist's impression of a projected mixed-power version of the I-185; the aft fuselage housed a pulse-jet engine acting as a booster.

**Data for the I-185 variants**

|  | I-185 M-90* | I-185 M-71 (etalon) | I-185 M-82A |
|---|---|---|---|
| Span | 9.8 m | 9.8 m | 9.8 m |
|  | (32.2 ft) | (32.2 ft) | (32.2 ft) |
| Length | 7.56 m | 8.05 m | 8.10 m |
|  | (24.8 ft) | (26.4 ft) | (26.6 ft) |
| Wing area | 15.53 m² | 15.53 m² | 15.53 m² |
|  | (167.1 ft²) | (167.1 ft²) | (167.1 ft²) |
| Empty weight | 2,068 kg | 2,709 kg | 2,437 kg |
|  | (4,560 lb) | (5,973 lb) | (5,374 lb) |
| Take-off weight | 3,223 kg | 3,629 kg | 3,328 kg |
|  | (7,107 lb) | (8,000 lb) | (7,336 lb) |
| Top speed at sea level | 604 km/h | 600 km/h | 549 km/h |
|  | (375 mph) | (372 mph) | (341 mph) |
| Top speed | 715 km/h | 650 km/h | 615 km/h |
|  | (444 mph) | (403 mph) | (382 mph) |
| at height | 7,300 m | 6,100 m | 6,470 m |
|  | (24,000 ft) | (20,000 ft) | (21,200 ft) |
| Climb to 5000m (16,400 ft) | 4.5 min. | 4.7 min. | 5.8 min. |
| Service ceiling | 10,250 m | 11,000 m | 11,000 m |
|  | (33,600 ft) | (36,000 ft) | (36,000 ft) |
| Range | 680 km | 800 km | 1,050 km |
|  | (423 miles) | (497 miles) | (652 miles) |
| Take-off run | 280 m | 300 m | 400 m |
|  | (919 ft) | (984 ft) | (1,312 ft) |
| Landing run | 355 m | 350 m | 350m |
|  | (1,165 ft) | (1,148 ft) | (1,148 ft) |

* Note: the performance figures for the I-185 M-90 in the table on this page are design estimates and such data for all models was with the engine on short-term boost.

Preliminary designs for the installation of the 2,200 hp (1,641 kW) M-71F were completed in 1943. An estimated top speed of 710 km/h (441 mph) at 6,250 m (20,500 ft) was calculated and, with a 21.5 m/sec (70 ft/sec.) rate of climb at sea level, the I-187 was expected to reach 5,000 m (16,400 ft) in 4.2 minutes. The engine cowling had rear sloping intake gills located between the propeller spinner and the front ring which had been moved back. The total effect gave the aircraft a more aerodynamically efficient shape. Further reduction in drag was achieved by synchronising the movement of the input and exit gills and by the new teardrop-shaped cockpit canopy; extra thrust was supplied by the use of ejector exhaust stubs.

The armament comprised two 20 mm ShVAK cannons in the centre section of the wings firing outside the propeller's arc and two synchronised cannons in the nose. There were facilities to carry eight RS-82 unguided rockets under the wings.

The **I-188** was the final projected version of the I-185. Had it been built it would have had the same armament as the I-187 but a different engine, the lighter but less powerful M-90, which also had the benefit of a smaller cross section.

The M-22-powered first prototype I-16 (TsKB-12).

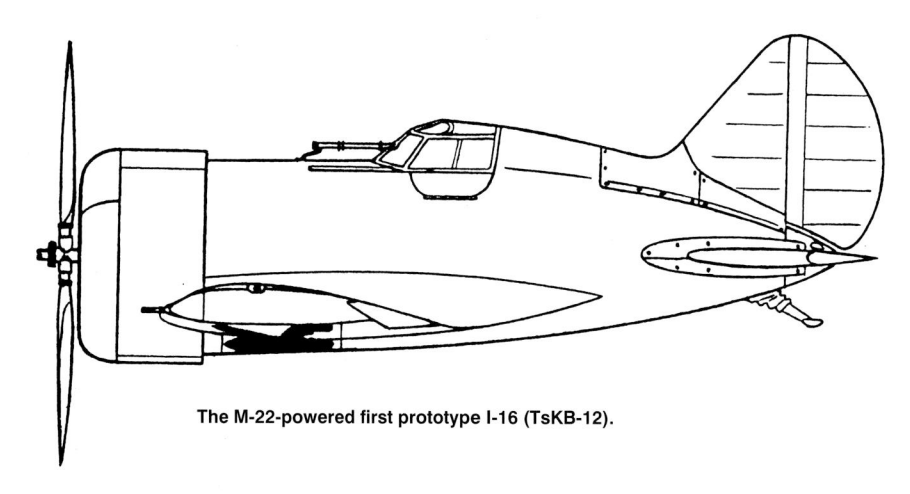

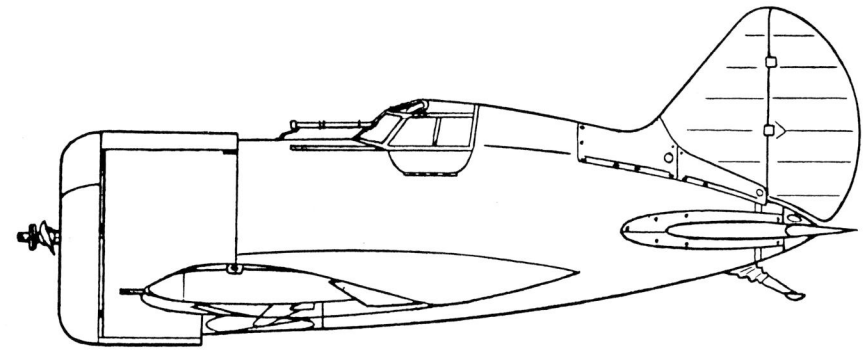

I-16 *tip* 4 (1934).

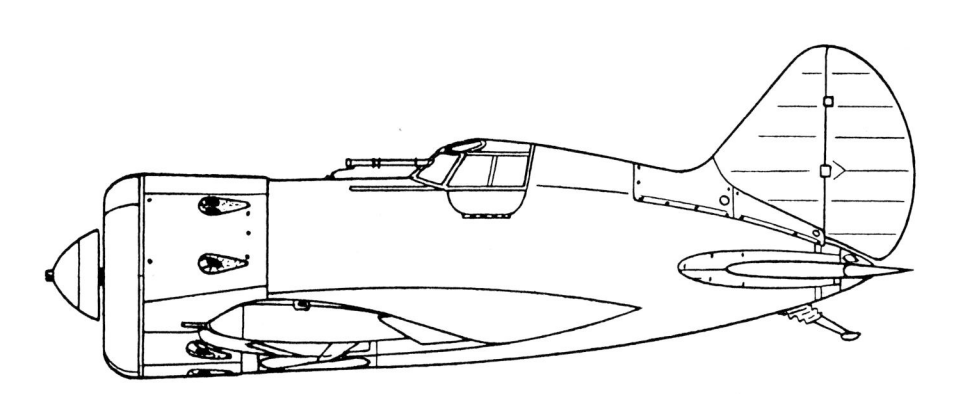

I-16 *tip* 5 (1934).

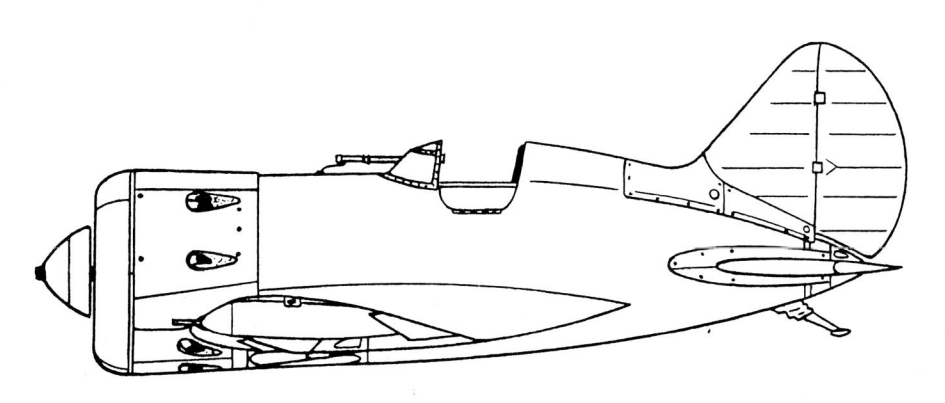

I-16 *tip* 6 (1937).

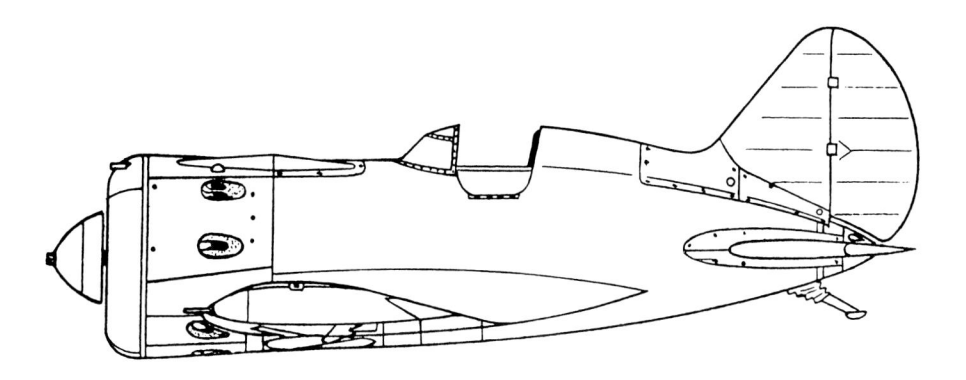

I-16 *tip* 10 (1937).

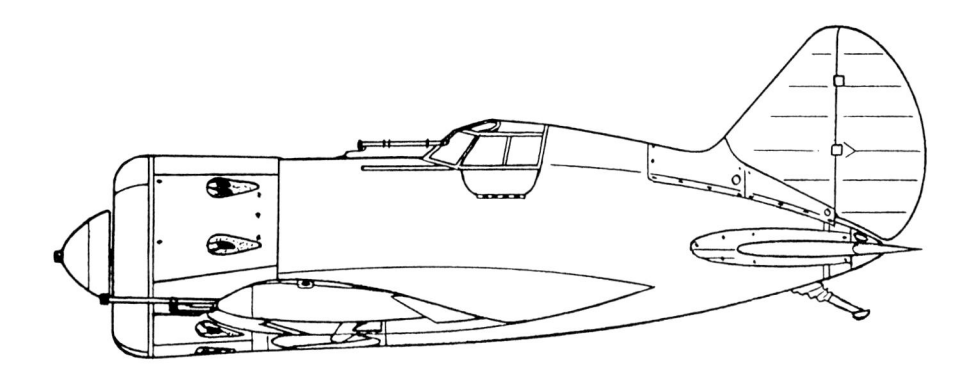

I-16 *tip* 12 (1936).

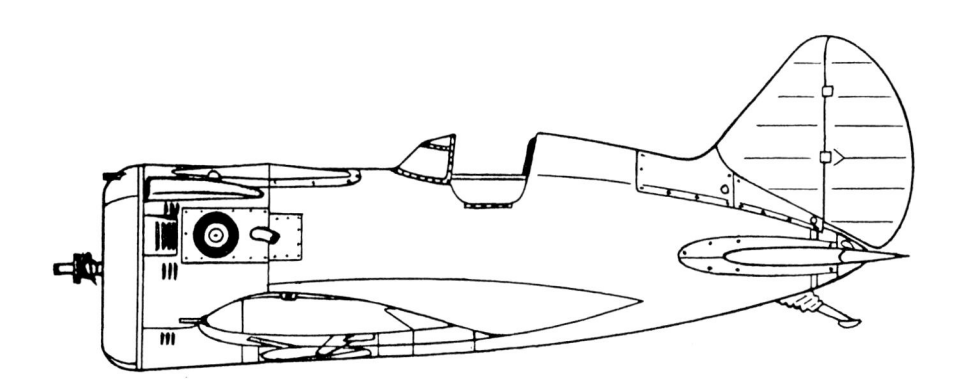

I-16 *tip* 10 (c/n 1021582) with TK-1 superchargers (1939).

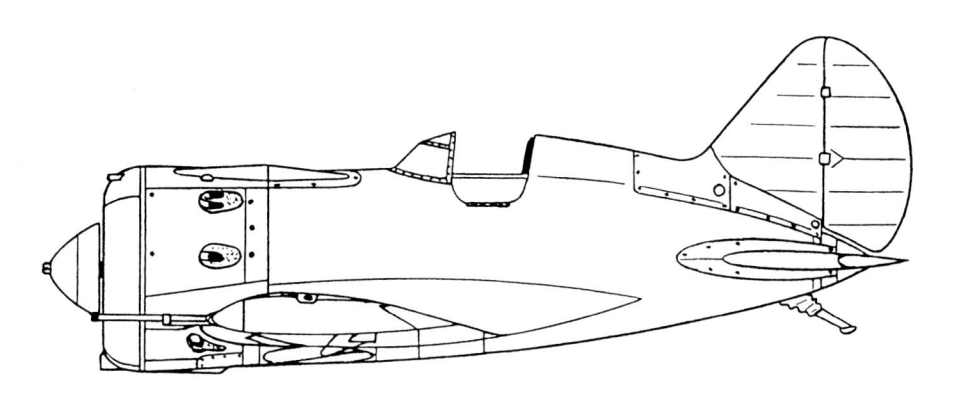

I-16 *tip* 17 (1938).

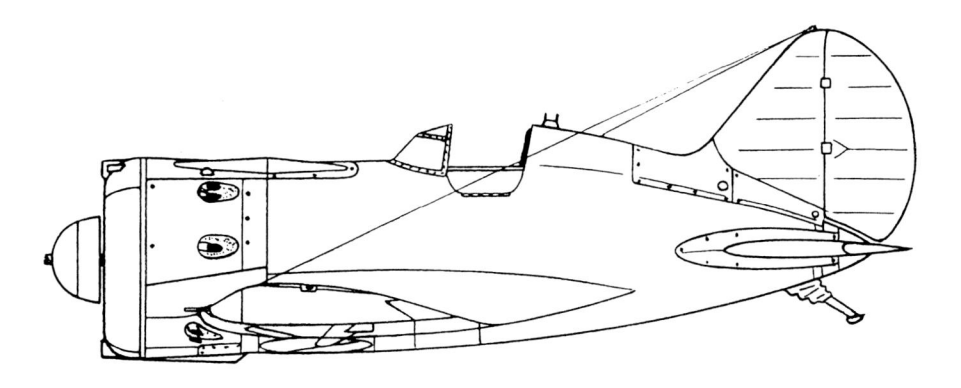

I-16 *tip* 18 (1939).

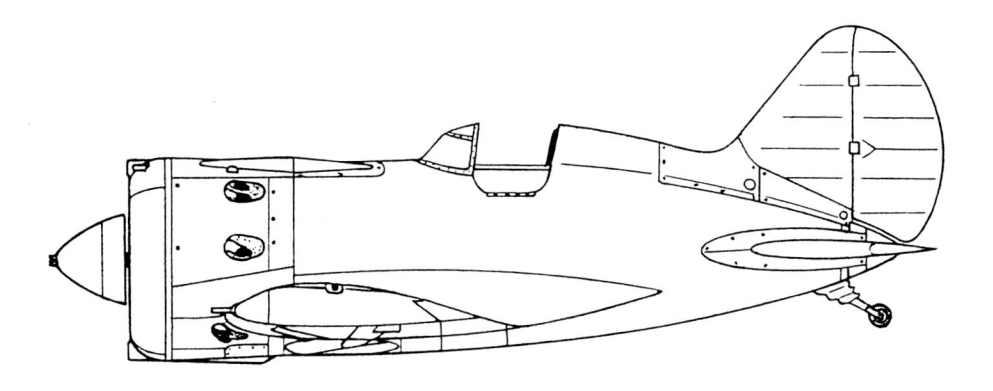

The prototype I-16 *tip* 24 (1939).

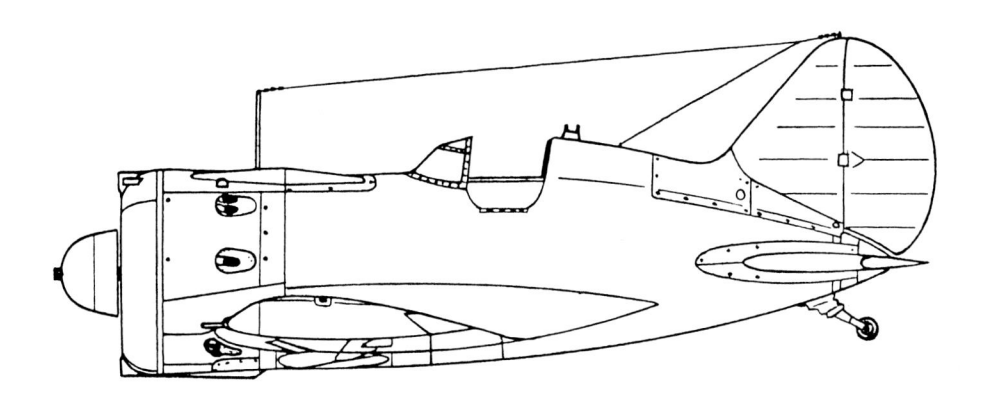

A production-standard I-16 *tip* 24 (1939).

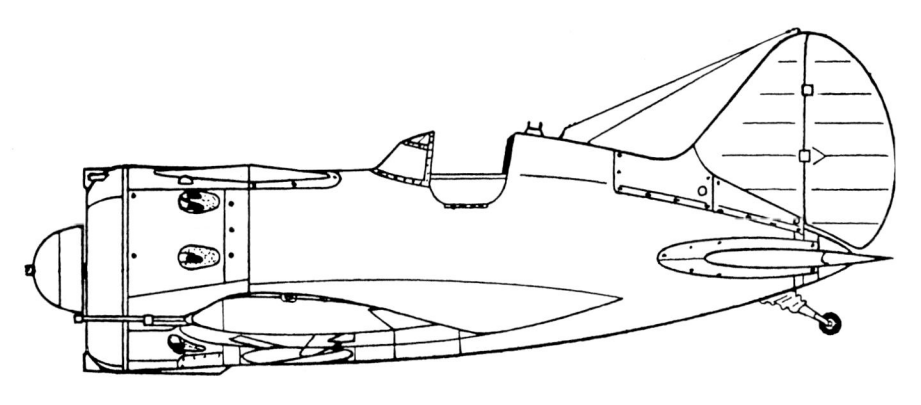

I-16 *tip* 27 (1939).

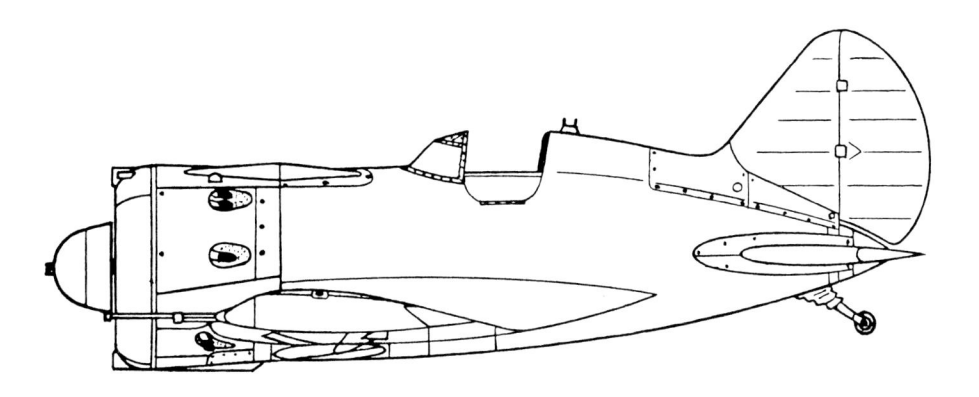

I-16 *tip* 28 (1939).

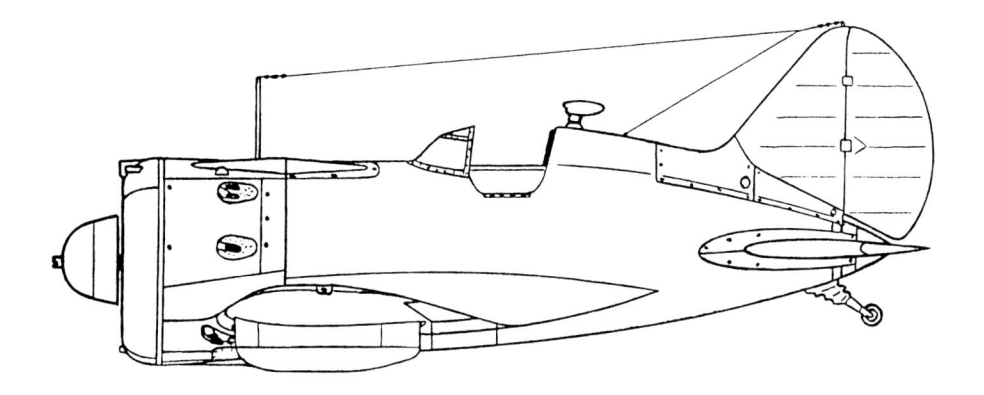

I-16 *tip* 29 (1940).

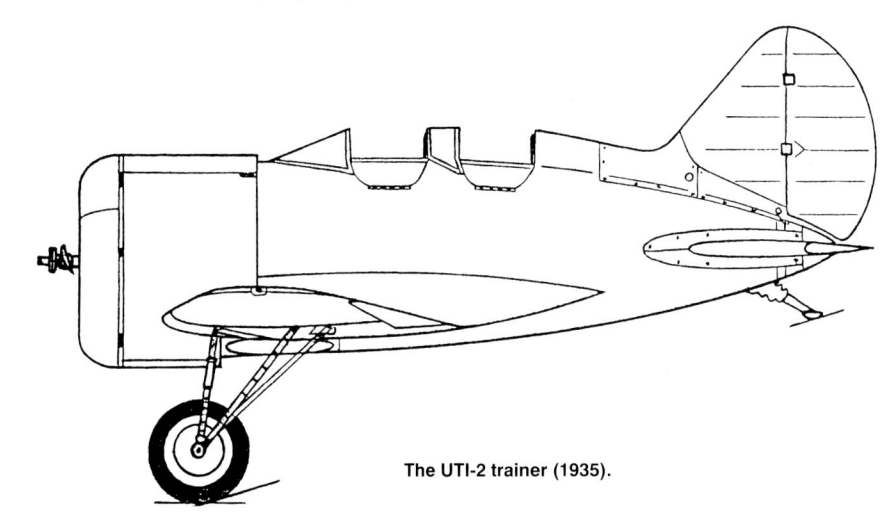

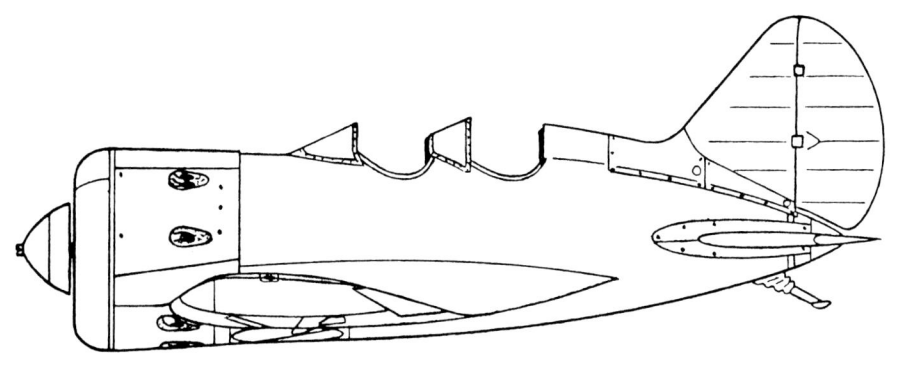

The UTI-2 trainer (1935).

The UTI-4 trainer (1937).

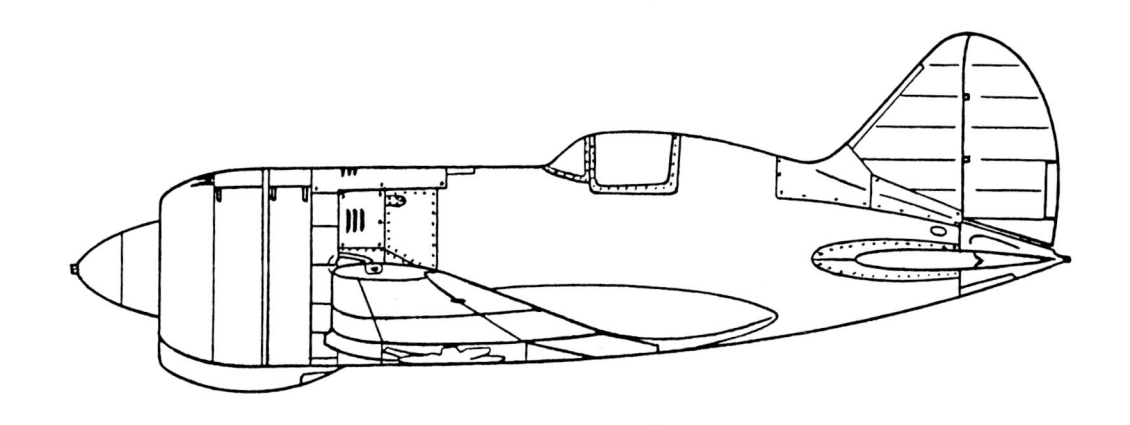

The third prototype I-180 (I-180-3) with enclosed cockpit.

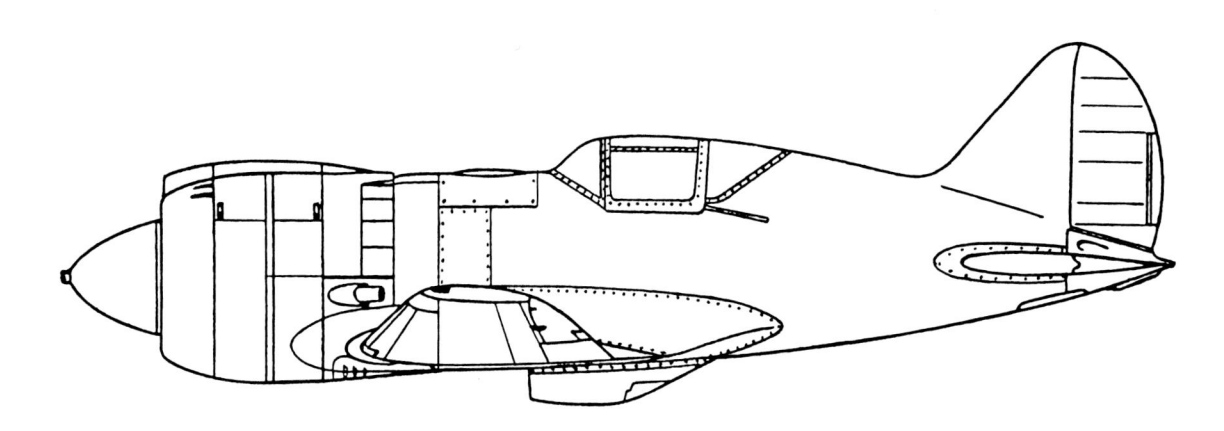

The M-71-powered I-185 (1941).

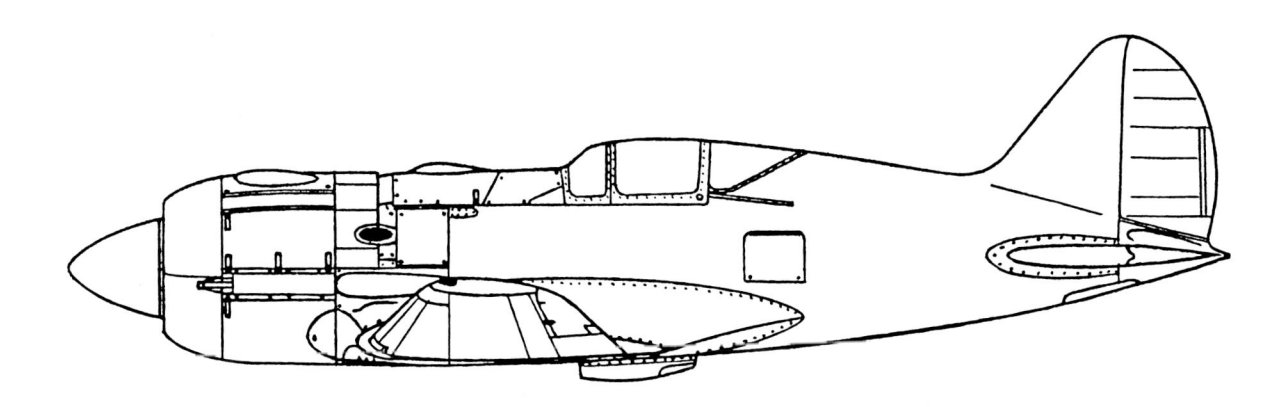

The M-82-powered I-185.

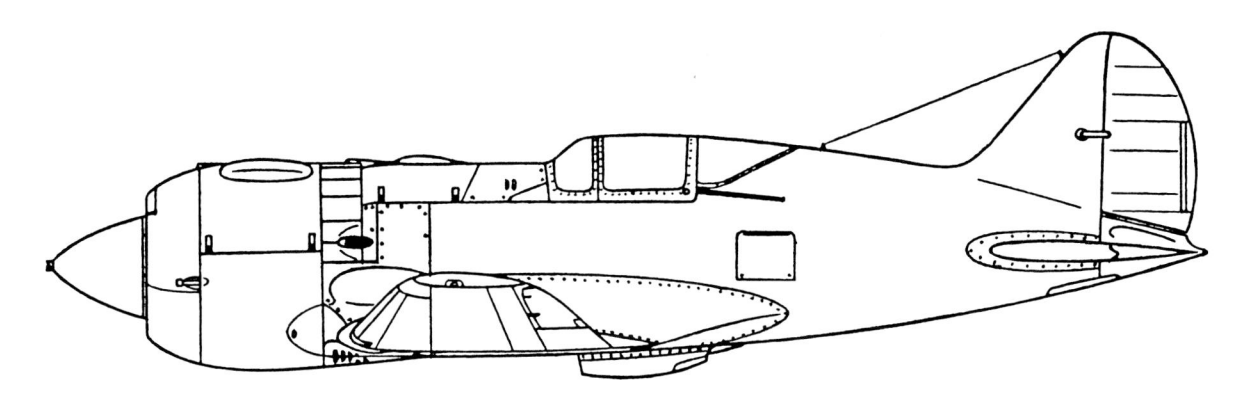

The M-71-powered I-185 *etalon* (production standard-setter) for 1942.

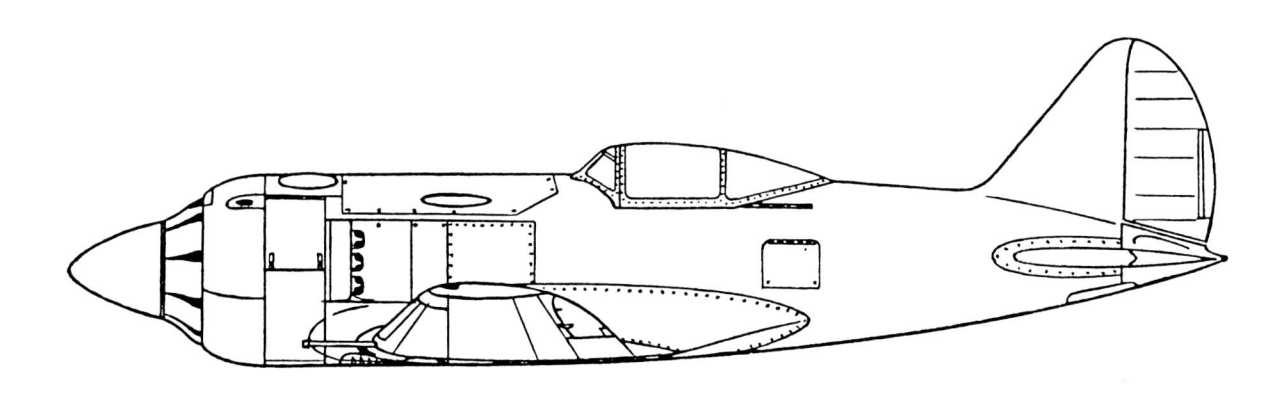

The projected I-187.

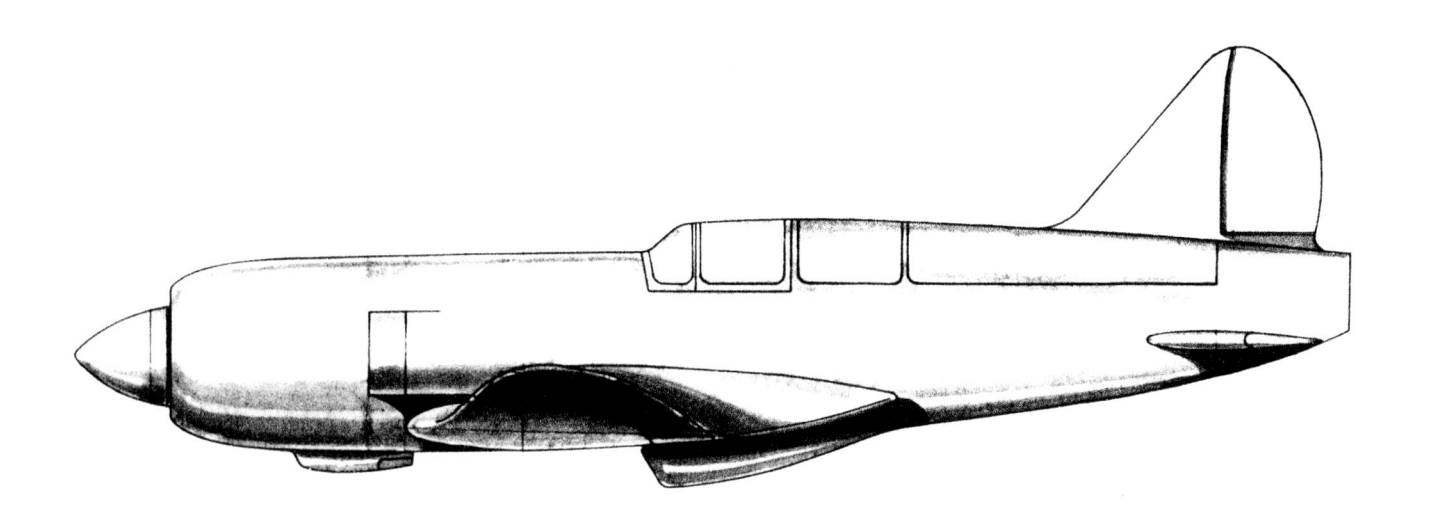

A projected mixed-power version of the I-185.

109

The ill-fated IL-400 prototype.

The first IL-400b before the accident.

The same aircraft following repairs, with modified engine cowling.

A production I-1.

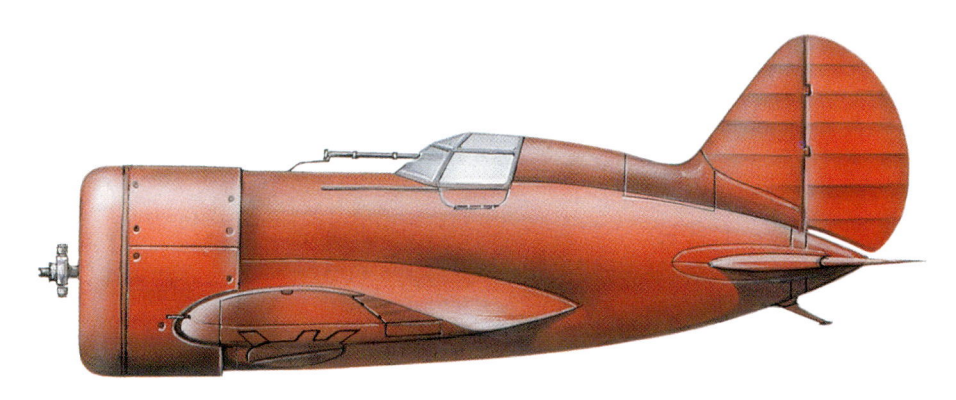

The TsKB-12 (first prototype I-16).

The third production I-16 *tip* 4 built by aircraft factory No. 39 (c/n 391203).

One of the standard colours schemes applied to production *tip* 4s.

The prototype I-16 *tip* 5 (c/n 391254).

111

Wearing this special colour scheme, this *tip* 5 was displayed at an aviation trade fair in Milan in the summer of 1935.

9 Red, a Baltic Fleet Air Arm I-16 *tip* 5 built by plant No. 39 (1939-40).

Flown by Lt. (sg) Boris N. Yeryomin, this I-16 *tip* 5 (7 Blue) was operated by the 160th Reserve IAP (Fighter Regiment) in June 1941.

An I-16 *tip* 10 operated by Yakooshev's display team.

**894 White**, a VVS RKKA (Red Army Air Force) I-16 *tip* 10 with an unusual three-digit serial.

The patchwork appearance of this *tip* 10 is due to the fact that parts from several other (probably wrecked) aircraft were fitted to make this one airworthy in field conditions.

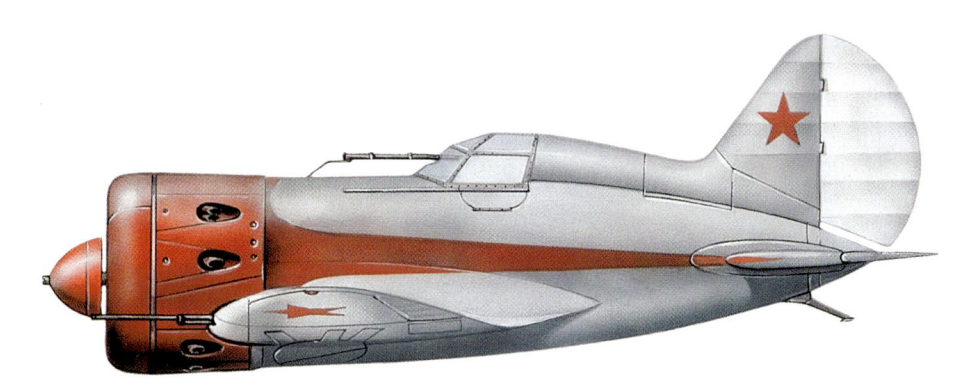

The prototype of the cannon-armed I-16 *tip* 12 (TsKB-12P).

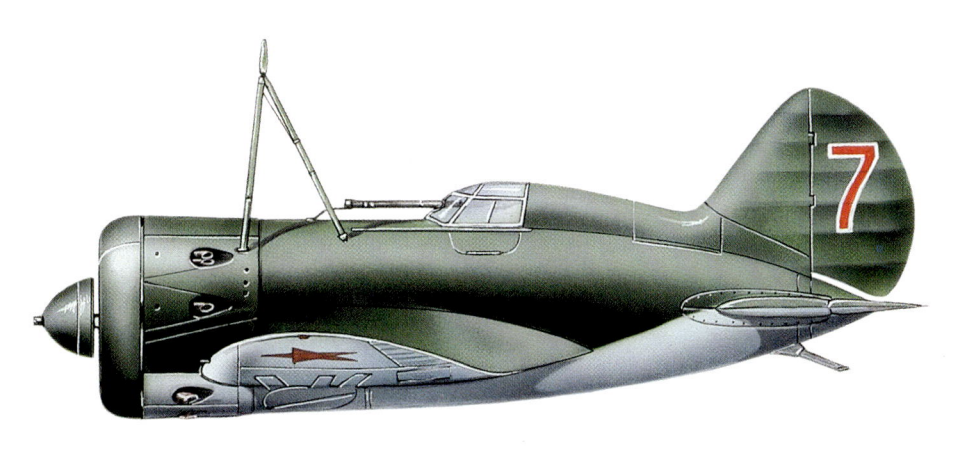

**7 Red**, a NII VVS I-16 *tip* 5 fitted with a non-standard aerial mast.

A Red Banner Baltic Fleet Air Arm/4th GvIAP (Guards Fighter Regiment) I-16 *tip* 10 flown by Lt. (sg) G. Tsokolayev (note Guards badge).

A standard *tip* 10 flown by VVS RKKA in the summer of 1941 with the air force badge on the tail.

This I-16 *tip* 17 serialled 7 Yellow was flown by 22nd IAP/3rd Sqn commander Lt. (sg) V. P. Troobachenko in late August 1939 during the war with Japan over Khalkhin-Gol River. Note the quick-identification fuselage band.

13 White, a camouflaged I-16 *tip* 18 of the 7th IAP, Leningrad Front, the autumn of 1941.

728th IAP I-16 *tip* 18 "91 White" operated on the Kalinin Front in the winter of 1942 in partial winter camouflage.

34 Red, an I-16 *tip* 17 flown by Lg. (sg) G. G. Gooryakov on the Leningrad Front in 1942.

This red-tailed I-16 *tip* 24 (3 White) defended Odessa in the summer of 1941.

A Baltic Fleet Air Arm/13th OAE (Independent Air Squadron) I-16 *tip* 24 with squadron markings, the summer of 1940.

I-16 *tip* 24 '33 White' was flown by 4th GvIAP squadron commander Vasiliy Goloobev (Hero of the Soviet Union) in October 1941 to June 1942.

This I-16 *tip* 24 operated by the 72nd SAP (Composite Air Regiment) in 1942 featured a gun camera. The fuselage slogan reads *Za Stalina!* (For Stalin!).

Another 72nd SAP *tip* 24 operated in 1941. This aircraft carried a *Za SSSR!* (For the USSR!) slogan.

'27 White/I White', a 254th IAP (Leningrad Front) I-16 *tip* 24 based at Boodogoschch and piloted by Lt. Krichevskiy in 1943.

This 72nd SAP I-16 *tip* 24 was flown by the famous ace Boris F. Safonov (HSU) in 1941. The inscription reads *Smert' fashizmu!* (Death to fascism!).

2 Red, an I-16 *tip* 28 operated in the summer of 1941.

This *tip* 28 carrying the slogan *Za Rodinu!* (For Motherland!) is unusual in having no propeller spinner.

The I-16Sh (I-16 No. 9211) ground attack aircraft.

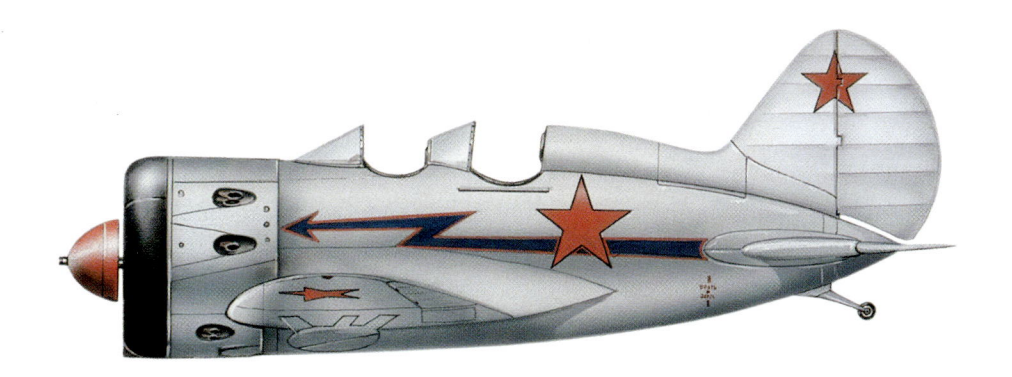

A North Fleet Air Arm/2nd GvIAP UTI-2 in an unusual colour scheme.

An UTI-4 operated with blind flying hood in 1943.

32 White, a 159th GvIAP UTI-4 with fixed landing gear.

The first I-16 *tip* 10 built under licence in Spain.

This rather drab *tip* 5 was based at Barajas in November 1936. It was probably aircraft painted like this which earned the I-16 the nickname *Rata*!

CM-110, a Spanish Republican Air Force/4a *Escuadrilla de Moscas* I-16 *tip* 6 based at Los Monjos with Popeye the Sailor artwork.

CM-158, an I-16 *tip* 10 with Betty Boop tail art. This aircraft was operated by the 1a Escuadrilla de Moscas at Liria in 1938.

CM-193, another *tip* 10 which defended Barcelona in November 1938.

9 Black, a Republican Air Force I-16 *tip* 5 in mottled camouflage.

I-16 *tip* 10 "23 Black" operating from Castellon in 1938 was unusual in having all-red outer wings and aft fuselage.

CM-225, an I-16 *tip* 10 operated by the 7a *Escuadrilla de Moscas* in late 1938, had an all-black forward fuselage.

This Spanish Republican Air Force tip 6 is inscribed *No tocan* (Don't touch). This warning was meant for their own pilots, not the enemy, indicating that the aircraft was under repair and was not airworthy.

CM 177, another 4a *Escuadrilla de Moscas* aircraft (I-16 *tip* 10). The Popeye artwork, which served as a squadron badge, differed considerably from aircraft to aircraft.

1W-1, an I-16 *tip* 5 captured by the Nationalists (1939).

This unserialled *tip* 10 was flown by the Nationalist Air Force's *Patrulla Azul* (Blue Patrol) led by Joaquin Garcia Morato in the spring of 1939. The unit badge reads *Vista, suerte y al toro* (Good sight, luck, and at the bull).

An unserialled I-16 *tip* 10 operated by the Nationalists' Fighter School at Moron.

1-W-22 of *Grupo* 26 illustrates the finish worn by Spanish I-16s in 1944-45.

C.8-41, a C.8 (I-16 *tip* 10) of the fighter school at Moron in post-war markings (1949). Note the non-standard bulletproof windshield.

C.8-25, another *tip* 10 operated by the same unit, had a mottled camouflage scheme.

This is how I-16 *tip* 10 CM-212 looked after being captured by the Nationalists in 1939; the offending red markings (and the serial as well) were immediately overpainted.

71 White, a *tip* 10 operated by the Chinese Air Force in 1939.

As the serial reveals, UT-1 was the first captured UTI-4 to be operated by the *Ilmavoimat* (Finnish Air Force). The aircraft flew with TLeLv 35 (35th Training Air Wing) in 1942.

Another war booty aircraft, an I-16 *tip* 29 evaluated by the Romanian Air Force. The aircraft was used for training fighter pilots in anti-I-16 tactics.

Coded DM+HD, this captured UTI-4 was evaluated by the *Luftwaffe*'s test centre at Rechlin.

31 White, a camouflaged Chinese UTI-4 (Chung-28A). Note that the national markings are carried on the wings only.

Captured Finnish Air Force I-16 *tip* 10 IR-101 operated by LeLv 30 in the spring of 1942.

A side view of the third prototype I-180 (I-180-3) as originally flown.

The second prototype I-180 (I-180-2).

The M-71-powered I-185 *etalon* for 1942.

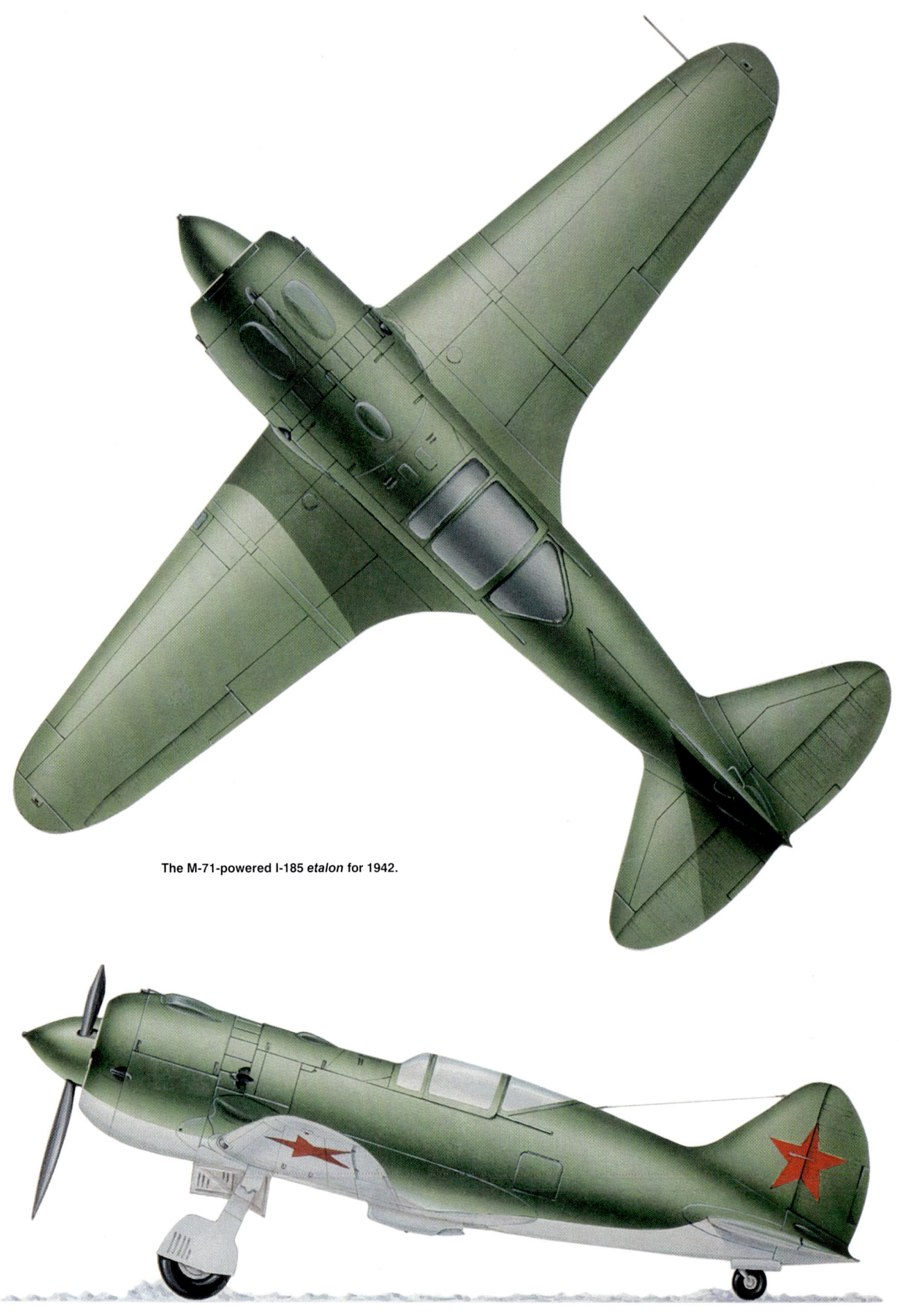

The M-71-powered I-185 etalon for 1941; note the difference in cowling shape.

5806, an I-16 tip 10, on display at the Chinese People's Liberation Army Air Force (PLAAF) Museum at Datangshan AB. The aircraft was restored haphazardly at best, with an absolutely non-authentic cowling and spinner, and the windshield is extremely crude, too.

UTI-4 'UT-1' on display at the *Suomen Ilmailu Museo* at Helsinki-Vantaa. This is the sole surviving UTI-4.

## We hope you enjoyed this book . . .

Midland Publishing titles are edited and designed by an experienced and enthusiastic team of specialists.

Further titles are in preparation but we always welcome ideas from authors or readers for books they would like to see published.

In addition, our associate, Midland Counties Publications, offers an exceptionally wide range of aviation, spaceflight, astronomy, military, naval and transport books and videos for sale by mail-order around the world.

For a copy of the appropriate catalogue, or to order further copies of this book, and any of many other Midland Publishing titles, please write, telephone, fax or e-mail to:

**Midland Counties Publications**
4 Watling Drive, Hinckley,
Leics, LE10 3EY, England

Tel: (+44) 01455 254 450
Fax: (+44) 01455 233 737
E-mail: midlandbooks@compuserve.com
www.midlandcountiessuperstore.com

US distribution by Specialty Press – see page 2.

### SOVIET X-PLANES
Yefim Gordon & Bill Gunston

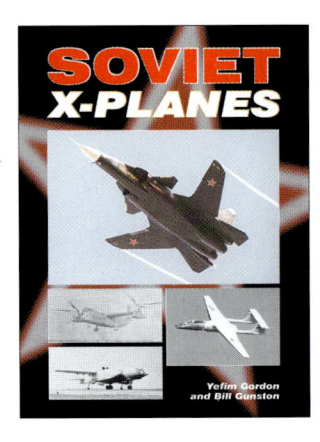

A detailed review of Soviet experimental aircraft from the early 1900s through to the latest Russian prototypes of today.

The book is the first to collect the stories of the more important Soviet experimental aircraft into one volume. Working from original sources the authors have produced an outstanding reference which although concentrating on hardware also includes many unflown projects. About 150 types are described, each with relevant data, and including many three-view drawings.

Hardback, 282 x 213mm, 240 pages
355 b/w, 50 colour photos; 200 dwgs
1 85780 099 0  **£29.95/US $44.95**

### Red Star Volume 1
### SUKHOI S-37 & MIKOYAN MFI
Yefim Gordon

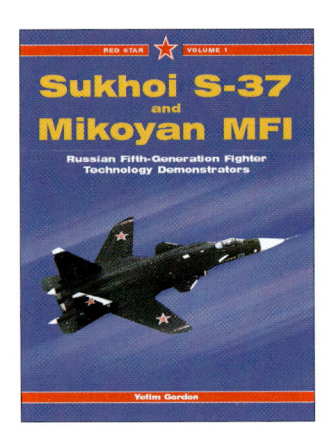

Conceived as an answer to the American ATF programme, the Mikoyan MFI (better known as the 1.42 or 1.44) and the Sukhoi S-37 Berkoot were developed as technology demonstrators. Both design bureaux used an approach that was quite different from Western fifth-generation fighter philosophy. This gives a detailed account of how these enigmatic aircraft were designed, built and flown. It includes structural descriptions of both types.

Sbk, 280 x 215 mm, 96pp, plus 8pp colour foldout, 12 b/w and 174 colour photos, drawings and colour artworks
1 85780 120 2  **£18.95/US $27.95**

### Red Star Volume 1
### FLANKERS: The New Generation
Yefim Gordon

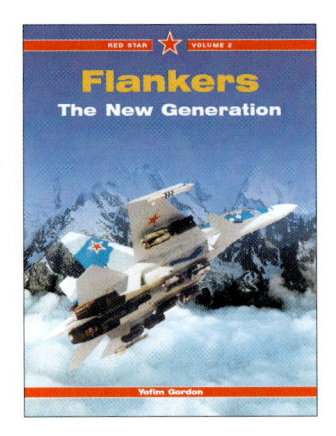

The multi-role Su-30 and Su-35 and thrust-vectoring Su-37 are described in detail, along with the 'big head' Su-23FN/Su-34 tactical bomber, the Su-27K (Su-33) shipborne fighter and its two-seat combat trainer derivative, the Su-27KUB. The book also describes the customised versions developed for foreign customers – the Su-30KI (Su-27KI), the Su-30MKI for India, the Su-30MKK for China and the latest Su-35UB.

Softback, 280 x 215 mm, 128 pages
252 colour photographs, plus 14 pages of colour artworks
1 85780 121 0  **£18.95/US $27.95**

### SOVIET COMBAT AIRCRAFT OF THE SECOND WORLD WAR
Volume One: Single-Engined Fighters
Yefim Gordon and Dmitri Khazanov

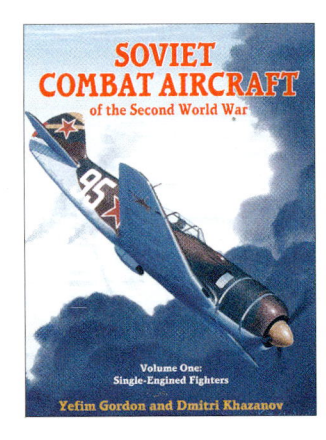

Arranged by manufacturer, this includes the prototype and operational products of famous designers such as Lavochkin, Mikoyan and Yakovlev as well as the lesser known, such as the Bereznyak-Isaev rocket propelled fighter.

Rich Russian sources including manufacturers, flight test establishments and Soviet air force and naval aviation records provide a wealth of new material, much of which rewrites previously held Western views.

Hardback, 282 x 213 mm, 184 pages
358 b/w photos; 28 layout diagrams,
16 full colour side views
1 85780 083 4  **£24.95/US $39.95**

### SOVIET COMBAT AIRCRAFT OF THE SECOND WORLD WAR
Twin Eng Fighters, Attack Acft & Bombers
Yefim Gordon and Dmitri Khazanov

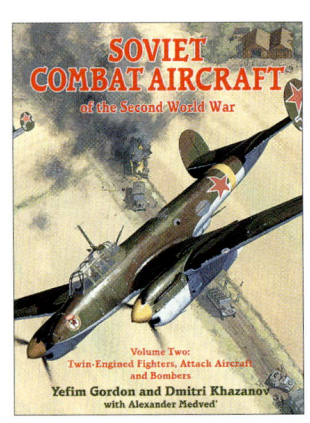

Arranged by designer, this includes the products of famous names such as Ilyushin, Petlyakov and Tupolev as well as lesser known types.

In his introduction, Bill Gunston explains the unique nature of Soviet aviation, the politics and strategies and the problems created by the vastness of the country – and confirms that the two volumes of *Soviet Combat Aircraft* are set to become the premier reference on this facet of aviation history.

Hardback, 282 x 213 mm, 176 pages
285 b/w photos; 27 layout diagrams;
17 full colour side views
1 85780 084 2  **£24.95/US $39.95**

### Aerofax
### YAKOVLEV Yak-25/26/27/28
Yakovlev's Tactical Twinjets
Yefim Gordon

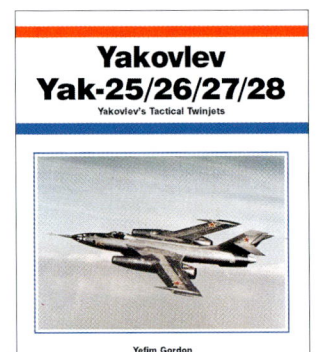

During the 1950s and 1960s the Soviet design bureau Yakovlev was responsible for a series of swept-wing twin-engined jet combat aircraft, all covered in this Aerofax – as usual with a mass of new information, detail and illustrations from original Russian sources.

Coverage includes the Yak-25 *Flashlight* flown in 1953, Yak-25RD *Mandrake* reconnaissance platform, Yak-26 three-seater, Yak-27 *Mangrove*, -27P *Flashlight-C*, and Yak-28 *Brewer*.

Softback, 280 x 215 mm, 128 pages
c180 b/w and c80 colour photographs,
drawings/side-views
1 85780 125 3  Dec 2001  **c£16.99**

### Aerofax
### MIKOYAN-GUREVICH MiG-17
Yefim Gordon

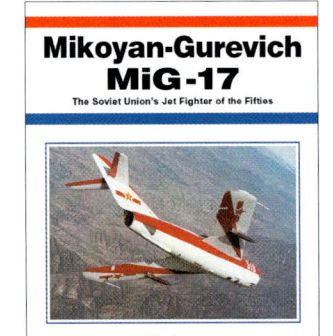

The Soviet Union produced and used around 9,000 MiG-17s. First flown in January 1950, it is an extensively upgraded MiG-15 with a redesigned 'scimitar' wing and lengthened fuselage.

It was built under various designations including the Polish Lim-5P and Lim-6bis and the Czech S-105, and served not only with the Soviet armed forces but with other Warsaw Pact nations, seeing combat in the Middle East, in North Vietnam and in Nigeria.

Softback, 280 x 215 mm, c160 pages
c130 b/w and c60 colour photographs,
colour sideviews, b/w drawings
1 85780 107 5  Feb 2002  **c£17.99**